RECOVERED

BY

HOPE

HELPING WOMEN RECOVER
FROM SEXUAL BETRAYAL

MICHELLE TRUAX

Published in Los Angeles CA, by Fireproof Ministries Inc.
Fireproof Ministries Inc. titles may be purchased in bulk for
educational, business, fundraising, or sales promotional use.
For information, please e-mail info@fireproofministries.com.

Unless otherwise noted, Scriptures are taken from The Holy
Bible, ESV, NIV, NLT and ISV.

English Standard Version (ESV)
The Holy Bible, English Standard Version. ESV® Permanent
Text Edition® (2016). Copyright © 2001 by Crossway Bibles, a
publishing ministry of Good News Publishers.

New International Version (NIV)
Holy Bible, New International Version®, NIV® Copyright
©1973, 1978, 1984, 2011 by Biblica, Inc.® Used by permission.
All rights reserved worldwide.

New Living Translation (NLT)
Holy Bible, New Living Translation, copyright © 1996, 2004,
2015 by Tyndale House Foundation. Used by permission of
Tyndale House Publishers Inc., Carol Stream, Illinois 60188. All
rights reserved.

International Standard Version (ISV)
Copyright © 1995-2014 by ISV Foundation. ALL RIGHTS
RESERVED INTERNATIONALLY. Used by permission of
Davidson Press, LLC.

The Library of Congress Cataloging-in-Publication
Data is on file with the Library of Congress
ISBN: 978-0692796818 (Fireproof Ministries)

This book is dedicated to every
woman who has been broken by
sexual betrayal.

It is for the warrior within her who
longs for healing and who will
stop at nothing to behold it.
It is for the women who have
boldly shared their stories with
transparency to offer hope to
those who would find themselves
here today.

You inspire me.

TABLE
OF
CONTENTS

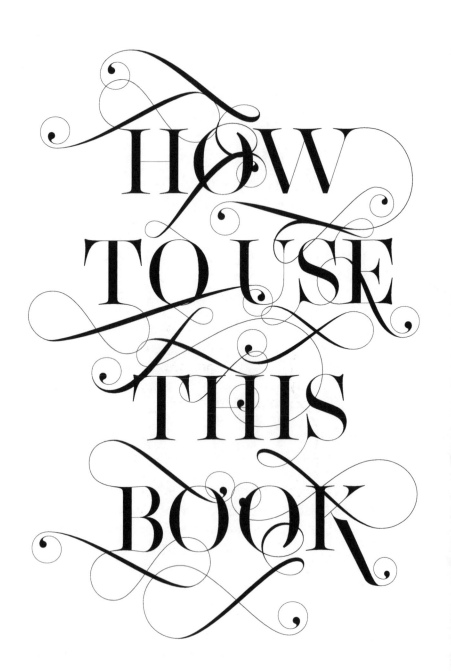

HOW TO USE THIS BOOK

Recovered By Hope is a compilation of letters from women around the world who have healed from sexual betrayal. Compiled by Michelle Truax, it includes her story of being married for over a decade to a man bound by pornography and sexual wrongdoing. Michelle shares her own journey, personal reflections, and the many successes and failures on the road to healing.

While this book was inspired and written to validate, uplift, and encourage, there is so much more available to help you at Recover.org. This book is a small part of what is included in the Recover workshop. Reading a book can be comforting, but we believe that true healing comes when one proactively pursues recovery through a series of action steps.

Carefully thought out and designed, the Recover workshop is made up of ten in-depth video sessions that take you from the discovery of betrayal, through the pain, and onto a path towards true healing. The workshop comes with an in-depth guidebook that challenges you through questions and practical exercises. You will learn to process your circumstances, thoughts, and feelings as you are guided in creating boundaries and your own personal plan of action.

Because we know that people tend to find healing through community rather than in isolation, we've created a small group online program specifically for women who need healing from sexual betrayal. These groups are facilitated by a trained group leader and are held privately through an exclusive online portal. You can learn more about the Recover workshop, guidebook, small groups online, and many other resources at Recover.org.

Lastly, Recover offers an exclusive retreat annually where women come away and find healing in the midst of beauty, friendships, rest, and relaxation. Consider joining us; rediscover yourself and all that you are meant to be. Learn more at Recover.org/retreat.

MICHELLE'S STORY

PART 1

To have finally arrived at this place where I can pen the thoughts that have been swimming in my head for over a decade is surreal. I've had many opportunities in my work with XXXchurch to speak to hurting women all over the world. Yet I longed for the opportunity to speak directly to you in writing-to share my heart, to help free you from some of the pain and confusion you may be suffering from right now as you hold this book. I want to share some of my story with you so you will know I *do* understand and that you are not alone. Even if our circumstances or backgrounds are different, the wounds of betrayal have brought us together. Betrayal is a sharp knife of deception and the cut it makes is deep. It comes in many forms, but one of the hardest betrayals to overcome is that of intimate and sexual betrayal.

I wasn't a stranger to betrayal. I'm a woman who has lived life from one end of the spectrum to the other. Raised in a single parent home in the 1970's without the influence or love of a father, but rather with rejection, abandonment, and a lack of love. My family wasn't known to be "warm". My mother was barely 20 and was wounded by her own childhood scars from a father who regularly used pornography, drank himself into an evil oblivion, and raged on his wife and kids. My mother, severely broken (and facing another rejection with my father splitting before I was born), did the best she could with the circumstances she found herself in. As for me, I didn't know any way other than the life that was laid out and displayed for me. I wasn't raised in the church and the world wasn't kind to me. There was neglect and sexual abuse and I longed to be loved, to be chosen, and to belong. I left home before the age of 16, unwed, pregnant, and full of shame. Crazy how history repeats itself. I spent years searching to find my place in the

world, all while raising a child I hoped wouldn't inherit the consequences of the generations before him.

I made many poor choices in the midst of some honest
attempts at good ones. It seemed natural that someone like
me was bound to end up on this road, married to a man who
would continually abandon and forsake me repeatedly for
three-dimensional images on a computer screen. I had been
told that wounded people don't make healthy choices and
seemingly I was caught between both. If you don't know love,
then you can only imagine that, when something feels or looks
like love, it is. Right? The old cliche of "looking for love in all the
wrong places" comes to mind. But, the truth is that it doesn't
matter what type of background or upbringing one has;
betrayal doesn't happen only to the weak, meek, or broken.
Betrayal happens to the smart, the funny, the educated, the
well-adjusted, the popular, the attractive, the wealthy, the
poor, the unattractive, the wounded, the healthy, the upright,
the righteous, the wayward and, well, any other characteristic
you can possibly insert.

When I met my husband, I was in awe of him. He was smart,
funny, talented, kind, had a good job, a good reputation, and,
bonus, he was handsome! I was the happiest I had ever re-
membered being around someone in all my life. We became
fast friends and spent hours upon hours talking on the phone
and sharing things about ourselves that allowed us to really
get to know one another before we entered into a relationship.
I was just on the heels of leaving a decade-long marriage that
had been riddled with all forms of abuse and misuse, which
left me feeling undesirable and extremely insecure. I wasn't
interested in entering into another relationship so quickly,

but this man just unexpectedly wowed my heart. He was the polar opposite of the abusive ex-husband I was finally free of. He learned of the rejections I had suffered in life and still outwardly valued and esteemed me. He also learned of the abuse in my first marriage and promised never to harm me. I truly connected with him in a way I had never connected with anyone before. We shared a love of books, music, life, spontaneity, and travel. We just clicked in so many ways and on so many levels. It was easy to be with him. It was comfortable, and I felt at home for the first time in my life. I believed with all my heart that God had brought him into my life.

But sadly, there was more to him than I could have possibly known. He was living a secret life behind closed doors. He had a deep and dark secret that only few who were closest to him knew; and even they didn't know it all. I did not come to know his secret until six months into the relationship, after I had fallen deeply in love with him. I had noticed that his moods were unpredictable. He would seem so agitated and angry over the most minuscule things. He'd go into a childlike tantrum over a knot in a shoelace or the seat in his car being adjusted and out of its norm. He would tell me for months I was the best thing that ever happened to him and then suddenly he would say things like, "You're too good for me. I don't deserve you." Because his mood swings were so severe, I seriously believed he needed to see a doctor—that there must be a medical explanation. Perhaps an imbalance or something that medication could help him with. That is when the truth came out. But not quite all of it. He told me just enough to be able to say that he told me. I was so naive.

As a boy, he had stumbled upon his father's stash of porn

-ographic magazines. He, his brother and some other kids found them and giggled over the pages, but they eventually got bored and wanted to go out and play like normal kids. Not him—he wanted more of the magazines. When life got hard (parents divorce and a move hundreds of miles from his father), he turned to the magazines for comfort. His mother remarried quickly and his step-father also had pornographic magazines hidden in easy-to-find places throughout their home. He was a tall, scrawny kid and was made fun of—heck even when I met him in his early 30's, his mother joked in the presence of many that he had a tapeworm. Nice, huh? His self-image was so twisted and broken that he found comfort in magazines that didn't talk back, that didn't tease, or ridicule. These magazines would give him a false sense of control and make him feel numb to the bullying and laughter he experienced from his peers. In his high school years when he finally met a girl and fell in love, she traded him in for a handsome, muscular varsity football player. As he experienced more and more heartache, an addiction was birthed and every painful event in his life became its food supply. And it grew and it grew and it grew.

By the time I found out, I was absolutely in love with him. His sweet and gentle spirit, his beautiful smile, his sense of humor, his iconic laughter. I had compassion and understanding and pure love for this delicate and incredible man. I had no idea that his addiction would rule him. I believed that love covered a multitude of sins. Twisting scripture to suit my situation became the norm as a result of my desperate desire to live life beside the man I loved. I naively believed love conquers all, that together we would would be better, that eventually marriage and the marriage bed would fix this. After all, I was attractive and in the best shape of my life. I was funny, strong, compassionate, kind, and I loved Jesus. Isn't that what we do? We think this is about us. That we have the ability to control the beast of pornography addiction in our loved one's life—or at least hold the potential to sway him back to reality. We think it's about looks or personality or something on the outside that these men are after, so if we possess those things then everything will be okay—or if we lack those things then it is our fault because, if we had them, then our men wouldn't need porn or other women!

The lies I believed for so long twisted and shaped my journey. It is my heart's desire to share the unfolded truths that I came to know in hopes of dispelling any lies you have embraced. My story as a wife married to a sex addict is a decade-plus-long rollercoaster ride of emotions from sadness and deep grief to anger and rage. There were seasons of compassion and grace, and there were seasons of anguish and bitterness. I learned a lot about this addiction, but greater than that was what I learned about myself and myself in God through it all.

If you are holding this book, I am going to assume it is because your heart is broken or because someone you care about is walking through despair from sexual betrayal. I understand what it feels like to have the bottom drop out of your reality and your dreams for the future rudely interrupted. I know what it feels like to wonder if it has all been a lie, if anything can be salvaged, or if you will ever be whole again. I also know what it is like to wonder if you deserved this or were just simply destined for it.

I've been the woman who sought desperately to help my husband more than he sought to help himself. I pursued help for his addiction from anyone who would listen. Pastors, counsel-ors, friends, certain family members, treatment centers, and online ministries. I remember feeling so hopeless because the addiction was prevailing and the broken cycle continued year in and year out. I have been blamed for my husband's addic-tion. I have been judged by my peers and family members, ridiculed by ignorant people, and abandoned by the church. I have walked much of this road alone and once stood in the midst of a pile of rubbish so suffocating that I wanted to stop breathing. Even in writing this to you now, it's hard to believe that hope was birthed in the midst of the most excruciating thing I've ever walked through.

That's the amazing news...there *is* hope and there is life after betrayal. Your circumstances will most likely be different than mine and your process of healing may look different too. Each of us is unique and recovery begins for each of us at different stages in our pursuit. There are so many facets to life and walking the road of suffering. Our backgrounds and experiences of trauma may be different, as is how we process it all.

How I longed for the day to write this book in hopes of help-ing women like you (and me) recover from sexual betrayal. I prayed over this book; I had an entire outline laid out for each chapter when it was interrupted by a thought that came to me—it would be much more beneficial for you to hear from more than one woman. Sure, I have walked this road and I can impart much wisdom from the things I've learned from firsthand experiences as well as my work at XXXchurch. I thought, wouldn't it be wonderful if I could gather a multitude of women in one place to share their heart with you, to give you hope, and encouragement on this road? That is how the idea came to make *Recovered by Hope* a compilation of letters from women, to women. To have a resource like this all those years ago when I went searching for help would have been comforting to say the least. There wasn't much out there for wives in 2002—let alone for girlfriends or fiancees.

Thankfully XXXchurch paved the way for churches to start talking about something no one wanted to talk about and now more than ever people are starting to realize what an epidemic pornography and sex addiction are, not just in the world, but also in the church. And, as you are very much aware—where there is a man bound by this addiction, oftentimes there is a woman who loves him and who bears much pain standing in the shadows.

Thankfully, throughout the years, I've met some extraordinary women who have also been down the road you find yourself on. They have pressed into healing and discovered within themselves a woman of great strength and courage. I've asked some of those women to sit down and write **you** a letter. A letter that would tell you something about their journey, what helped them, what didn't help them, and where they are today. Each of them felt honored to share a piece of their heart in order to help you process the situation you find yourself in today.

These are not letters of endorsement, nor am I agreeing or disagreeing with everything in them. I am not offering them as advice to you, but rather to give you **hope and encouragement.** These are the experiences of other women and the conclusions they came to for themselves as well as

RECOVERED BY HOPE | *Michelle's Story Part 1*

about their relationships. Remember: your circumstances may be different and there may be some letters that don't even seem to apply to you and that is okay. There are letters here that are written from the different perspectives of women whose marriages survived as well as from those whose marriages didn't. Letters from women who discovered the betrayal before marriage. Letters from women whose experiences differ even though the betrayal is the same. There is something in here for everyone. If you come upon a letter that doesn't apply to you, may I encourage you to move past it and keep reading, as there is sure to be one or more that will speak to your heart. Grab a cup of warm tea and a box of soft tissues. Let the love these ladies have for you embrace you. May you be encouraged and inspired, but most of all may you find *hope*.

REJOICE GREATLY,
DAUGHTER ZION!
SHOUT, DAUGHTER
JERUSALEM!
SEE, YOUR KING COMES TO
YOU, RIGHTEOUS
& VICTORIOUS.
RETURN TO YOUR FORTRESS,
YOU PRISONERS OF HOPE;
EVEN NOW I ANNOUNCE
THAT I WILL
RESTORE TWICE
AS MUCH TO YOU.

-Zechariah 9:9,12 NIV

{ YOU ARE
SO MUCH
MORE
THAN HIS
MISTAKES }

With the bombardment of airbrushed magazine covers at every grocery checkout and only the most elite featured on reality housewives television shows, it is no surprise women struggle with self-image. This is all the more greatly compounded for the woman married to a man who pursues pornography and/or other forms of sexual gratification outside of the marriage. Cynthia knows all too well what being married to a man who struggles with sexual sin can do to his wife's self image.

DEAR LOVELY ONE,

Through a journey of pain and tears, this is redemption to me, to my story. To write you this letter and let you know that you're not alone in this journey.

First off, I want you to know that you are enough! You are beautiful and valuable, and there is so much more beauty for your life and your marriage than the ashes you are now experiencing. Be hopeful, beloved, because redemption is at hand.

Redemption may look differently in each of our stories. Sometimes it looks like reconciliation and sometimes it doesn't, but regardless of where you are in your journey, know that it will be redeemed. This journey has taught me so much about myself, like nothing else ever did. I have discovered a strength I never knew I had and an endurance I never even dreamed of. You see, the very thing that should've left me bitter and angry has polished me. Has brought the gold out of me that I didn't even know was there. My dear friend, do not let your husband's choices determine your identity. You are so much more than his mistakes.

I remember when I first found out. I had immense feelings of shame, guilt, and insecurity. I felt like somehow it was my fault and that I wasn't good enough. I was ashamed of my body, of my face. I would belittle myself by believing that I couldn't compare to the physical beauty of the women my husband looked at in porn. Anytime we were intimate, I found myself trying to compete with these women, only to feel like an object and a fake. I'd cry every time, unable to connect with him or have true intimacy because I always wondered if he really wanted me or was fantasizing about these women. All these thoughts would haunt me, leaving me drained and depressed. I hated him for that. I resented him for not protecting my heart like he promised on our wedding day.

After years of torturing myself with these thoughts, I allowed God to heal me and restore my heart. My heart felt so broken, I couldn't take it anymore. I remember God's love feeling so tangible during that season. God demonstrated His love for me and time and time again he'd remind me that my identity was in Him and not my husband.

I began to work on me. So many years had been so focused on getting my husband help that I was lost in translation. There were fragments of me that felt like ruins that would never experience their glory days again. To my beautiful surprise, those ruins are now pillars of the woman I am today. I began to love me again. I began to see the beauty in me and the value of being an image-bearer of the King of kings! I no longer felt broken and depressed. Now don't misunderstand me, I still felt the pain of betrayal, but I no longer felt responsible for it.

The closer and more intimate I'd get with God, the more identity He spoke to me. I found myself again and I loved it. I remember once telling my husband that I no longer compared myself to the women in porn; instead, they couldn't compete with me. I was enough and I was the real deal and if he couldn't see that, then he would lose a valuable gift God had entrusted him with. This was when he began to get it. I think this new confidence he saw in me encouraged him to walk in intimacy with God to find his identity in Him and not in his mistakes.

As my husband continues to walk his journey, his freedom and sobriety don't determine mine. I can't guarantee that he won't relapse along the way, but I surely know where I stand in the process. I've put my trust in the One who will protect my heart.

Though the journey to freedom is long and painful, celebrate each day, beloved. Celebrate you and celebrate the victories as they come. Celebrate your breakthroughs and your dreams. Each day is a new gift and a new opportunity for you to heal and be restored. Get to know you and love you right where you are.

**WITH MUCH LOVE,
CYNTHIA**

To watch more of Cynthia's story, visit Recover.org.

O ISRAEL,
HOPE IN
THE LORD!
FOR WITH
THE LORD
THERE IS
STEADFAST
LOVE, &
WITH HIM
IS PLENTIFUL
REDEMPTION.

-Psalm 130:7 ESV

{ **THE POWER OF GRACE** }

Like many of us, Christina dreamt about what life would be like once she was married and had children of her own. The ultimate happily ever after. She believed that marrying a pastor was safe and ensured her security for a marriage of integrity and fidelity. What she learned instead is that marriage isn't always about security and fairytale endings, but rather about grace, forgiveness, commitment, and vulnerability. Ultimately she learned how to be transformed through the pain of her reality.

DEAR FRIEND,

I feel a tremendous sense of honor and privilege to be able to share my story with you. I believe that when we share our stories with honesty and vulnerability, we begin to release the hold that brokenness has over us. Instead, it build bonds that will support us in our journey to recovery. As I have prayed over these words and considered the ultimate goal, I know that my story is wrapped with grace. Of all the lessons I've learned in my life, the power of grace has been the strongest and most defining.

When I close my eyes, I can vividly see myself as a child playing in my room. Barbie and Ken dolls strewn across the floor; love; weddings, marriage, family life in full-blown play. My imaginative play only had room for happiness, love, and fairytale endings. As I grew older, life faded from pretend play to real love, and I began to realize that life wasn't always about happiness, love and fairytale endings. It's about grace, forgiveness, commitment, vulnerability, and learning to love yourself as God loves you. He ultimately brings the fairytale ending. There are so many things that I learned along my journey, but the most important thing I learned is to love myself- in spite of my situation and in spite of my husband's addiction. His actions cannot, do not, and will not define who I am, and I hope that you discover that as well.

From the beginning, what I desired most from my marriage was to feel that my husband would fight for me. More than half of my married life I wondered—no, *worried*—that I would do something, make a mistake or somehow not be enough and he would choose to walk away. His attitude and inability to be present constantly sent me a message: I was not worthy of his fight. In a lot of ways, that damaged me more than anything during his addiction. During the beginning of his recovery, I had a difficult time trusting his heart, motives, and love for me. But, over time as words became actions, trust was rebuilding. As God began to heal my husband, he was able to begin to see the damage that his actions had caused and he began the process of reclaiming my heart. He humbled himself in the face of the devastation that his addiction caused, taking full responsibility for his actions; not shying away from my tears, my anger, my need for moments of silence or distance. He honored me with his words, acknowledging my pain as well as my strength, in both private and public. He took genuine interest in finding ways to show me how much he looked forward to spending time with me, planning date nights, and engaging in the moment.

As I reflect on my greatest heartache during that time, I am in awe that I am no longer the woman who longs for a man who will fight for her and that I feel assured that my husband is the pursuer of my heart. That God placed a call on his heart and he responded to it. I am in awe of the magnitude of a God, who worked to recover and restore the heart of my husband and that by His grace we were able to restore our marriage. I am fully aware that had my journey taken a different path-had my husband and marriage not been restored-that my God would still have been there, ready and able to restore my heart, as the one who pursues me like no other.

There will be times during your journey, as you may have already experienced, when you will feel that anger is the emotion you know best. I remember those days. I wish I could tell you that I only embraced grace and kindness, but this journey is hard and there are times when anger is needed to help you move through the journey and grieve the loss of what you thought you had. The thing is, anger doesn't have to be your home—you can choose to be in charge of your actions and reactions. I admit, there were times when I lost sight of that fact and had to find my way back to who I am. I had to make the daily decision to be in control of my emotions for myself and for my daughters. Those decisions not only helped my recovery, but also ensured that my daughters had the mother they needed me to be; not broken, but restored. I hope that, wherever you find yourself in your journey, you know you have the power to recover your emotions.

I wish for you: recovery, healing, and a life full of the love that God has designed you for. We may not know each other by name, but I am praying for you. We both have a story and we both will be victorious!

**BLESSINGS MY FRIEND,
CHRISTINA**

To watch more of Christina's story, visit Recover.org.

REJOICE

IN HOPE,

BE PATIENT IN

TRIBULATION,

BE CONSTANT

IN PRAYER.

-Romans 12:12 ESV

{ ALLOWING
GOD INTO
MY PAIN
CHANGED
EVERYTHING }

During turbulence, it is hard to stay calm. I know when I am on a plane, the minute fierce turbulence hits, my body immediately responds by becoming tense. I have to tell myself that it won't last forever. In a sense, I have to walk myself through the fear so that I can intentionally relax my body and come to a place of peace. Jenna knows all too well what it felt like to experience turbulence in a marriage affected by pornography. She also knows how to experience peace in the midst of a storm.

DEAR FRIEND,

I sit here, years after discovering my husband's betrayal, thinking of everything I wish someone had told me when I first found out about my husband's porn addiction. I would begin with, "It is not your fault..." I know how personal it feels. I understand not feeling good enough, comparing yourself to others, or wanting to judge every person who might catch your husband's eye. It hurts.

If I could sit with you now and hear your heart, your pain, your grief, and sorrow, I would. There is nothing so precious as being heard in the midst of your pain. I want to encourage you to do something that I did as I was healing: get a journal, find a solid support group, and get it out.

Share your story, your pain, your fears. I sat and wrote out my pain to God in prayers and shared in a private online forum. There was nothing so freeing as getting it out, talking it through, and allowing God to speak to my heart in the midst of all my pain. He would whisper what my heart needed to hear and friends would speak truth and life into me. While this did not change my circumstances, it did change my perspective.

I found that I had put my husband on a pedestal where he did not belong. My husband was never supposed to become my idol; nor was my marriage to be my security. My security is in my God, who promised never to leave nor forsake me. (Joshua 1:5, Hebrews 13:5)

I also had to work through my own wrong thinking. I remember one time saying, "Once a cheater, always a cheater." And in that moment, the Lord whispered to my heart, "Who are you to say what I can or cannot do? I am the judge, not you. It is not your place to say someone cannot change." It took time to sort through all of the turbulent emotions I was feeling and frankly, time for the Lord to speak His truth to my heart. I did not always want to hear it. There were times I fell to pieces, into His arms and just cried. And truthfully, I am so grateful I did. There is nothing so comforting as the God of the universe assuring you that you are loved, you are wanted, you are beautifully made, you are enough.

There were many moments, in my pain, that I wanted to rage. I wanted to cruelly throw my husband's sin in his face to prove the pain he caused me. I wanted him to hurt as I hurt. Turning to God in those moments, wanting to be justified, He gently spoke His truth. The truth is that I will, one day, stand before God, equally needing Jesus, alongside my husband. I am no better than he. We both need forgiveness. We both need His grace. This sounds like a simple place to arrive, but when you are in the thick of it, it can be hard to swallow. It is hard to walk in the hurt someone else has caused, repeatedly. It is also hard to admit that you are just as sinful.

In my healing, I knew my husband was not the enemy. Too often, pain begets pain and wrong choices make their mark, affecting so many areas. People wind up choosing what will numb the pain. Some choose alcohol, some drugs, some hide, some work more than needed; anything to ignore or dull the pain. Many choose porn to meet that need.

Porn brings shame. Shame drives people to hide, to justify, to minimize the offense, or to lash out. People respond in different ways, but the root is the same. And the answer is no different. For me, allowing God into my pain changed everything. It did not change my circumstances; it changed me. I no longer take my husband's actions as personal, though I *know* it feels very personal to so many of us. I can walk in grace and mercy because I have been shown grace and mercy and God asks for no less than extending what we have been given. (This is *not* the same as blind trust or forgiveness with no boundaries, that is not wisdom.) I can walk in peace, knowing that even if the *worst* happened (for me, it was being abandoned), I would be okay because my hope is in God, not in any human being.

My healing did not happen overnight. The truth is, it took time and intentionally seeking healing. The truth is it took years. It took honesty with myself, my husband, and with God. It also took active steps to rebuild the trust that was crushed under the weight of his sin. I want to encourage those of you at the beginning of your healing journey. As you step into the darkness of the pain, know the sun is coming on the horizon of healing. It is always darkest before dawn. Healing will look different for each person, but the Healer is the same.

I can truly say that I no longer fear a 'fall.' I no longer check his history fearing the worst. I no longer expect the worst. My husband is not the culmination of his sin and neither am I. I share this to say that while this crisis feels like it has shattered your world forever and you will never be okay again, it hasn't. There is hope that it will not be the primary thought on your mind or worry in your heart forever.

There is hope for you, for your marriage, and for your family.

I cannot promise an outcome, but I can promise you can find peace in the midst of the storm. Isaiah 26:3-4 says, "You (God) keep him in perfect peace whose mind is stayed on you, because he trusts in you. Trust in the Lord forever, for the Lord God is an everlasting rock."

I want to encourage you to do the best thing you can do for yourself right now—invite Jesus into the most painful places and ask Him to speak to your heart, allow Him to meet you in it and speak life into you. He is the God of all comfort (2 Corinthians 1). He can be trusted. He knows your pain. "Cast all your cares on Him because he cares for you." (1 Peter 5:7)

I am praying for you to abound with wisdom, grace, and mercy; that you would find healing in forgiveness, regardless of the outcome.

Seek peace and healing in the middle of your circumstances. Seek the Healer.

**BLESSINGS,
JENNA**

To watch more of Jenna's story, visit Recover.org.

FOR I KNOW
THE PLANS I
HAVE
FOR YOU,
DECLARES
THE LORD,

PLANS TO
PROSPER
YOU & NOT TO
HARM YOU, PLANS
TO GIVE YOU
HOPE & A FUTURE.

-Jeremiah 29:11 NIV

{ WALK
OUT OF
YOUR
SHAME }

Many of us experience encounters with people who say careless things out of ignorance or worse, judgment. Connie was one who endured many years of pain, but found a way to walk out of her shame and she lovingly encourages you to do the same.

DEAR FRIEND,

Imagine that I am sitting with you while having lunch in a quaint little restaurant with the commotion of others' voices filling the air. We quickly open up the secret places of our hearts to each other because that is what women like us do. We are in a sisterhood we never dreamed possible or would ever have chosen. We will both look around to ensure our own safety as private pain pours from our hearts. I lean forward, intently listening to your every word while watching your tense facial expressions as you attempt to convey the heart-wrenching pain of your husband's betrayals, held deeply in your soul. I want to wipe away the stinging tears as they leave streaks on your delicate face, but refrain so you can maintain the rhythm of your story. You may instinctively lower your eyes away from mine because shame has likely surfaced while you consider how no one could possibly understand your pain. You will catch yourself unable to breathe while feeling naked and exposed and I will attempt to do what I wish others could have done for me while in my darkest of days- I will purposely lift your beautiful face in my motherly hands and speak tenderly to your soul by saying:

"Sweetheart, I hear your fears, your familiar and desperate plea for answers and the first thing I want you to know is you are in a safe place to share your deepest secrets. Please know that you are not alone because I have been right where you are."

The second truth I will want to sear into your mind is this:

"Dear one, you are not crazy. This is not your fault. You did not cause his sexual addiction and you cannot change it. Your husband's sexual addiction says nothing about you, yet very much about him. It is the system he chooses and has likely chosen to deal with his pain, long before he knew you."

Our wise SA Counselor released me from my shame that so many others had burdened me with by their careless words. Their message of, *"If you would just try to be a better wife by being more sexual, less critical, more submissive, and less triggering, your husband wouldn't struggle with sex addiction,"* left me so confused. These comments are not only damaging, but are also complete fallacies that will only prolong an addict's acting out, thus hindering his recovery. The more I quieted my voice and amped up my praises of him, the more freedom he felt to act out because he knew I had bought into their lies and was taking a false responsibility for his addiction. Being gracious and forgiving in the early stages of his recovery is complex and unfortunately Christians push this agenda because they believe it will appease the addict and quiet you. Showing tough love and setting firm boundaries for yourself, while having a strong support system made up of others who respect your values, will achieve more than you could ever imagine.

I was fortunate to be in a healthy support group with a graciously skilled facilitator who did not over spiritualize my situation. Most importantly, she never accused me of being co-dependent, a co-addict, or in any way responsible for my husband's addiction. We worked hard on issues surrounding my safety, anger, grief, and eventually, after my husband had maintained some sobriety, issues around the intimacy in my marriage. This was imperative for my own growth as well as my husband's recovery. My husband and I also had an incredible counselor that believed the responsibility was solely on my husband not only to be sober, but also to repair the horrific damage he had propagated in our relationship. He demonstrated to my husband how to better protect my heart while teaching him how to demonstrate true empathy. Because of this, I found healing and the strength to forgive and eventually he was successful in regaining my trust. This process in our marriage is still ongoing and may take many more years to feel truly safe.

My hope for you is a glorious restoration. I wish it were possible for you to pray all this trauma away, but you will have to fight on all levels; spiritually, emotionally, and physically. Your husband will also be unable to pray his way out of an addiction he behaved his way into and will need to understand the underlying emotional issues that have been a catalyst for his addiction.

Walk out of your shame when choosing to stay or leave your marriage. After much prayer and when you feel certain that he isn't moving toward recovery after you have given him ample time and grace to do so, then and only then, can you decide when enough is enough. Leaving your marriage can be as loving as staying because neither the choice to stay or to leave is braver than the other. If you know you are called to stand firm in this battle for your marriage, then do not let anyone tell you he isn't worth fighting for. This is your life and your marriage, not anyone else's. You alone will have to live with the choices you make. Your counselor, your pastor, your friends, and your family will not be the ones living with the consequences a divorce promotes.

Be at peace, sweet sister, while remembering that this life is but a breath compared to eternity. Also, if we don't have the privilege of meeting on earth, one day please look for me in heaven as I will likely be holding up a glittery pink sign that says: *"Calling all brave women (who chose to love) to come over here for a great big group hug!"*

IN HIS ABIDING LOVE,
CONNIE

To watch more of Connie's story, visit Recover.org.

MAY THE GOD
OF HOPE FILL
YOU WITH ALL
JOY & PEACE AS
YOU TRUST
IN HIM,

SO THAT YOU MAY OVERFLOW WITH HOPE BY THE POWER OF THE HOLY SPIRIT.

-Romans 15:13 NIV

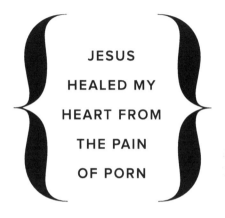

{
JESUS
HEALED MY
HEART FROM
THE PAIN
OF PORN
}

Blindsided by her husband's confession of pornography use, Katie was left feeling duped for having been a "good girl"—someone who saved herself for marriage. It took her some time to work through the betrayal and to witness her husband's repentance and journey of recovery. Through it all came new opportunities and experiences that have forever changed her and her marriage for the better.

DEAR FRIEND,

So be strong and courageous! Do not be afraid and do not panic before them. For the Lord your God will personally go ahead of you. He will never fail you nor abandon you. (Deuteronomy 31:6 NLT)

I know you are going through a pretty rough time right now! I've been there and many times I felt alone. No matter what the outcome of your relationship, God is with you and will never leave you.

My story was slightly different than most because my husband confessed his addiction to me. I truly felt alone when he told me. I didn't know who to talk to or even what to say. I felt so betrayed. I played by the rules. I had saved myself for my wedding night and now three years into our marriage, I learned porn was part of his life. I thought he could just stop watching porn and life would resume back to normal. The questions of what was wrong with me filled my brain. Through the process of healing, I now know that it had nothing to do with me. Since my husband has found freedom, I have to say that our marriage is amazing! We had a good marriage before, but now it is more than I ever could have imagined. Jesus healed my heart from the pain of porn.

I want to offer you hope. Hope that God works all things together for those who love Him. When we were in the mess, I certainly didn't see any good that could possibly come out of this addiction. Through my healing heart, God gave me a love only Jesus can give for the women who work in the sex industry. This might sound crazy to you, but I am involved in a local Strip Church chapter that goes and shares the love of Jesus with women in strip clubs. I also attend porn conventions with XXXchurch and love people as Jesus did—right where they are. I'm not saying He will work in the same way in your life as He did in mine, but He will see you through this healing process.

As a mom, this addiction has opened my eyes to the dangers my children face. We are very careful of what our kids watch. I do my research before we see a movie. I am always more concerned with the suggestive sexual content than a few in-appropriate words or violence. Our kids don't go on YouTube. My eyes have been opened and I can't ignore the fact that kids have the opportunity to be exposed to porn at a much younger age in the digital world. I will do all I can to break the cycle of porn addiction in this family.

As you continue on this journey to find healing, I want to en-courage you to find someone to talk with. You need to be able to share your heartache, challenges, and struggles with some-one. Stay strong! We have the hope of Jesus who will never leave our side!

**WITH LOVE,
KATIE**

AND SO, LORD, WHERE DO I PUT MY HOPE?

MY ONLY HOPE IS IN YOU.

-Psalm 39:7 NLT

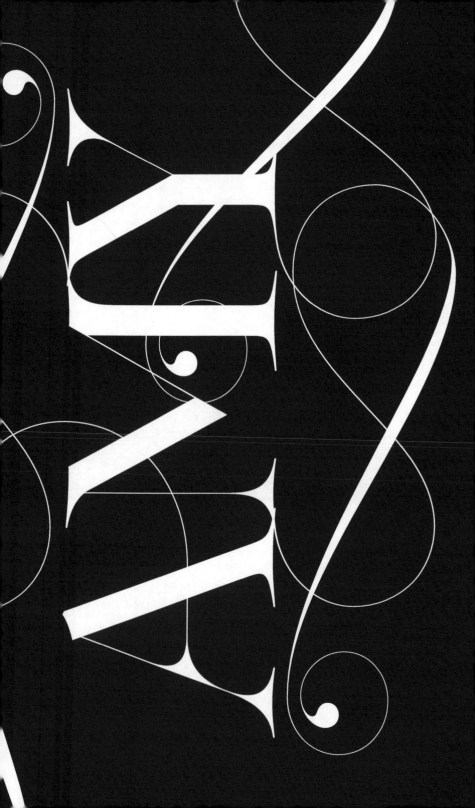

{ YOUR FEELINGS ARE COMPLETELY VALID, SWEET SISTER }

Wounds from childhood affect many of us. Some of us have entered into marriage just as wounded as our spouse. We're thrown (and rightfully so) by sexual betrayal because it affects us on such a personal and intimate level. Yet it can actually be the catalyst to bring about a deep and much-needed healing within us if we allow it. Amy knows firsthand exactly what that looks like and perhaps that is why she was so open to the thought of extending mercy and grace to her husband as well as a willingness to work through it with him as he journeyed towards his own healing. Let Amy's fun way of communicating some hard things be a breath of fresh air for you today.

MY DEAR FRIEND,

I have been where you are. We are different people and our circumstances aren't identical, but I know how the wind gets knocked out of you when you discover that the one you love has been neck-deep in porn. I am so sorry that you are having to go through this. If you will, please allow me to share with you a bit of hard-earned perspective. I don't buy into the "*time heals all wounds.*" I believe that Jesus heals all wounds, but time affords us much-needed perspective.

I surrendered my life to Jesus at the age of 23, two weeks before my eldest son was born. I was pregnant and alone. I was not entirely sure whose child I was pregnant with (my husband's or the man with whom I had been having an affair) and I came within minutes of aborting my unborn child. (P.S. I grew up in a Christian home and we never missed a Sunday at church.) The earthly father I knew was angry and absent. The earthly mother I knew had no joy and suffered from chronic depression. How many of us know that broken people raise broken people? Can I get a witness? (I always tell my kids that they will work it all out in counseling *chuckle.*)

I had never seen any evidence of a present, loving God—let alone one who just plain got a huge kick out of me because I am His. One who wanted to be near me so badly that it pleased Him to crush His Son (Isaiah 53:10). One who sings over me because He delights in me (Zephaniah 3:17). One Whose thoughts toward me outnumber the grains of sand, all the grains of sand (Psalm 139:18). When I began to learn about that God, I fell deep and hard for Him. He didn't tolerate me; He chased me. He wasn't indifferent toward me;

He chose me. He wasn't disappointed in me; His delight is in me. He doesn't despise my weak humanity; He utilizes my weakness as a doorway to display His power. It truly was His kindness that led me to repentance. He heard my weak cries from the pit of shame that I was in and lavished me with kindness, love, forgiveness, and peace. And I never looked back. God's kindness and love have been ever-present through all seasons of my life.

Despite many declarations that I would never marry again, six years later I married an incredible man, he adopted my son and we went on to have another two sons. He, inexplicably, thinks I am the most beautiful woman there ever was and is not afraid to tell me that all the time. For the 17 years that we have been married, he has been emblazoned in a battle against porn addiction. Actually, the porn addiction has been around a whole lot longer than I have been in his life, I just didn't find out about it until after we were married.

If I had pages and pages, I would fill them with the up's and down's of our journey together. The way I started out as his "cheerleader," absolutely positive that, if I just prayed fervently enough, he would kick the habit. I hated him, loved him, felt compassion, and despised him—sometimes simultaneously. I tried threatening, crying, screaming. I tried ignoring and passive-aggressing (is that a verb, y'all?). Over the years, I have moved in and out of anger, grief, indifference, depression (dude, Zoloft was my friend), interest in sex waxing and waning, near-misses (on both our parts) in regards to extra-marital affairs. Him because porn doesn't always stay neatly on the computer screen; and me because my heart was lonely and primed for someone to come along and talk to me, hear me, love me.

There have been seasons in which I have screamed at the Lord and informed Him that the only reason I was not leaving my husband is because I promised Him that I would stay. I also made it clear in those conversations that I was choosing GOD and NOT choosing my husband. I was staying because, well, I just wasn't released. Again, this is my journey. Only God knows the intentions and heart of a man and has already lived all of his days. God is not formulaic in His dealings with us. He restores. He rebuilds. He provides. Should you stay or go, know that reconciliation is the very language He speaks. Here's what I know about addiction—it is medication for our hurting hearts. Our deep down, broken parts. We ALL have something that soothes us. I guarantee you have something that you turn to in times of anxiety. I have always loved Jesus, but food is my drug of choice. In my family of origin, we eat when we're happy, sad, angry, celebrating, grieving, and everything in between. It's been my friend in the evenings when I am lonely. It brings only momentary relief, but it has been there since I was a child. What do you medicate with? Spending/shopping? Exercise? Pills? Television? Food? Sex? Movies? Books? Booze? Video games? Pornography? Social Media? Pinterest (#Jesustakethewheel!)? It is important that we recognize that addictions are habitual medication for pain; a way to momentarily "check out" of life when it gets overwhelming. Some of these addictions have consequences that are much more far-reaching, but in the end, they all simply start out as a means to find a moment of relief and they are all roadblocks to living a life of complete peace and joy.

This is not, in the least, to diminish the pain and feelings of betrayal that we experience when we discover that our husband has been looking at an army of naked women/men online. I mention these things to simply bring the panic down a notch so that we can think clearly and reason that we all have something that we turn to. You've heard this before (and it is 100% true): his porn habit has got nothing to do with you. Your feelings are completely valid, sweet sister. Completely. In fact, we have to feel in order to heal and it sucks. The Lord shared this passage in Philemon with a friend of mine years ago as she and her husband were walking through this same scenario and it has never left me. When Paul was sending Onesimus back in among a dear group of believers after he had been "useless" to them, he appealed to the group to be accepting of Onesimus. Now, pretend for a moment, that this is the Lord speaking to you about your husband. Please do insert your husband's name as you read it—it wrecked me when I did.

"I could be bold and order you to do what you ought to do...I prefer to appeal to you on the basis of love...I appeal to you for My son, _____; formerly, he was useless to you. I am sending him—who is My very heart—back to you. He is very dear to me...welcome him as you would welcome me. If he has done you any wrong or owes you anything, charge it to me...I will pay it back—not to mention that you owe me your very self." (Philemon v. 8-12, 16-19, NIV, emphasis added)

Notice that none of this negated or diminished the wrongdoing, but simply acknowledged it. And in our scenario where it was the Lord speaking to us on behalf of our husbands, we are told to charge it all to Him and He will repay it. This is consistent with the Lord's promise that He will, "Repay you for the years the locusts have eaten." (Joel 2:25) "Who but the Lord can repay lost time?! He can do it, I tell you! He is close to the brokenhearted and saves those crushed in spirit." (Psalms 34:18, NIV) "He collects every, single one of our tears in a bottle." (Psalm 56:8, NLT). You are seen and heard and pain matters to Him. Your husband's pain matters to Him.

It is also important to remind ourselves that our husbands are not evil—our fight is never against flesh and blood (Ephesians 6:12). Our husbands (along with everyone ever) are part of Jesus' reward for His suffering. He deeply loves them all—as much as He loves you!

On a practical level, I am going to tell you that being hyper-vigilant did not work for us. I am not meant to be my husband's main accountability partner and I have found that all of my super-sleuthing always led to nothing but more heartache for me. One of the most effective things I have ever done is join with two other dear and trusted girlfriends of mine whose husbands were also fighting this battle. Once a week, come hell or high water, we met together for two hours. The only rule we had in place was that we could not talk negatively about our husbands. Holy moly. That was not easy. We would sincerely pray for them, for our kids, and for healing in our hearts and marriages. We would force ourselves to state—out loud—one thing we were grateful for. Is the only thing you can think of, "He keeps the bed warm at night?" That's totally valid. What about, "He works so I can stay home with our kids?" Totally valid. "He grills a mean hamburger?" Absolutely! It didn't have to be flowery or "sound Christian," but it had to be authentic. A grateful heart will always, always be the starting point for forgiveness and sincere prayer. Every time I have ever done that, it's usually no time at all before the gratitude begins to snowball and I remember that I have some "legitimate" bigger things to be thankful for. When we would do that, suddenly my husband was not the worst ever.

Here is my best advice at this juncture:

1. Your husband is not supposed to be your source; God is your one and only able Source. People are supports—that's it. If your identity is wrapped up in your husband, ask the Lord to show you how to derive your true identity from Him. Ask Him for revelation of who you are.

2. Pray like crazy for the Lord to intervene in your marriage and in your family. Keep on praying and ask others to pray.

3. Find a good counselor, even if you have to go alone. If you are a sexual abuse survivor, many times porn and adultery are high-trigger areas and you may even experience some degree of PTSD-like symptoms when you discover your husband's addiction. In this case it is imperative that you seek a good counselor to help you through that added layer of suffering. Don't just go to a counselor when things have tanked. Keep a good one around and have a "check-in" a couple times a year. We all go to the dentist twice a year, for goodness' sake.

4. Get with one (preferably two) others who are walking through this season and learn to worship and pray authentically from a seat of grief. Your pain is not only an acceptable offering to put on the altar for the Lord, but a beautiful one and one He greatly treasures. When you feel empty and that you have nothing to give, offer Him your pain. We generally have that in abundance.

5) Be honest with the Lord. I talk to Him like He's right next to me. I dump it all in His lap. He knows every word before it's even on my tongue, so why not just let it all out? It breeds intimacy with Him, friend. Be real with the Lord. I cannot overstate. Drop the church-y crud and Christian-ese. Just speak plainly to your Father who adores you and is already in tomorrow with every last thing that you need to survive (and thrive in) that 24 hours. And the next one. And the next one. All of them.

6) "Give it to the Lord" has always sounded a little too ethereal for me. I prefer to just "tattle" to the Lord. Seriously, tell on your husband. I journal—it's how I pray most of the time. I dump any and all things—especially hurts—right at His feet. All your life you've been told "don't tattle," but I assure you, the Lord wants it all. It doesn't have to be rational: if it matters to you, it matters to Him. That, my friend, is how you "Give it to the Lord." Tell Him how you feel. It creates room for Him to fill you with peace and give you hope for another day.

7) Forgive, forgive, and then forgive again. It will free you.

I wish I had a magic formula to share with you. What I know is I love my husband, but I love God more. I keep choosing the Lord and the more I back off and stop trying to control the situation, the more I see the Lord effectively working on my behalf. Life is a marathon, not a sprint. Your husband is going to trip and fall, as will you. Love is intentional and a choice. Porn is not the thing; the pain it is medicating is. Seek hard to discover that pain and ask the Lord to bring His Truth. Ask Him to show you the things that the enemy does not want you to see. If you choose to stay, it will be hard and it will be beautiful. If you choose to go, it will be hard and it will be beautiful. Either way, God cannot be unloving and He cannot be unkind and He cannot be unfaithful. He will work in you an understating—if you lean hard into him in your pain—that there is great purpose in pain and you will encounter facets of Him that you would not ever get to see if you choose to run from Him when you hurt.

LOVE,
AMY

FOR IN THIS
HOPE WE WERE
SAVED. NOW
HOPE THAT
IS SEEN IS
NOT HOPE.
FOR WHO HOPES
FOR WHAT
HE SEES?

BUT IF
WE HOPE
FOR WHAT
WE DO NOT
SEE, WE WAIT
FOR IT WITH
PATIENCE.

-Romans 8:24 ESV

{ I WEPT AT
THE ALTAR &
TOLD GOD I
COULDN'T DO
IT ANYMORE }

Stereotypically it is men who want sex, sex, and more sex. And women, apparently according to the beliefs of many, we just do it to appease our husbands. That couldn't be farther from the truth for many of us or for Tiffany. She shares how bitter and angry she became that her husband could easily self-gratify, while her sexual needs and desires went unmet. So much so that she became the "porn police."

DEAR SISTER,

I am so blessed to be able to share a small piece of my journey with you. I wish that I had an instant, magic formula that was guaranteed to work for you and your marriage. The truth is, this will take a while and it is not easy. You are so brave for taking this first step! Learning how to be supportive of my husband, choosing daily to love him and show him grace was an ugly, messy, painful process.

For 12 years, I was the angry, bitter, resentful wife. I was filled with self-doubt, blaming myself for not being attractive enough for him. I have always had a high sex drive, so I couldn't understand why he needed more. I was also a little jealous that he could satisfy himself whenever he felt like it, but that I often felt as though I was begging for sex. I enjoyed having sex with my husband, but often felt like he wasn't really present or that he was just fulfilling an obligation. I can't even begin to count the number of nights that I cried myself to sleep. I spent years as the porn police, searching for evidence to disprove his lies.

It wasn't until I finally let go of my marriage and gave it to God that true heart changes began to happen. I wept at the altar and told God I couldn't do it anymore. I have never stopped loving my husband, but I couldn't handle the lies, betrayal, pain, feelings of PTSD, or fake apologies any longer. God revealed to me that I needed to pray for my own reactions while He worked on my husband's heart. Ephesians 4:29-32 became my mantra. I want to share the prayer I prayed over him daily before he woke up and several times during the day: *"Lord, I lift my husband up to you. Shield his eyes, protect his heart and deliver him from temptation. When he is tempted* today Father, I pray that he would take the way out that I know you will provide. I pray that these struggles will strengthen our marriage, not destroy it so that we can share our victory and glorify you. Amen"

I was literally ready to walk away, but we made it through with God's grace, accountability software, tons of prayer, lots of open, honest, uncomfortable conversations, and sharing our struggle with our pastor. God has turned our misery into ministry and we now walk alongside couples as they learn to fight the battle together, instead of battling with each other. One of the most important things I could say to you is to be prepared for a relapse. Set boundaries and be ready to enforce them. I was blindsided after almost a year of sobriety and had no plan.

I have so much more of my story that I want to share with you, but I'll leave you with this. Pray continually...pray for God to heal you, to give you strength, to show grace, to protect your husband, and to heal your husband. Do not let yourself be consumed by his choices; we can only control our reactions to their actions. Don't be the porn police; help him find an accountability partner you can both trust so you can intentionally focus on loving him. Make sure that you love yourself—you need rest, energy, and a lot of self-care! When you are ready, help him re-train his brain. Share long, loving kisses daily, make love with the lights on, look into each other's eyes during sex and give each other non-sexual, full-body massages. Most importantly, know that you are not alone and that I am praying for you daily!

BLESSINGS,
TIFFANY

SURELY THERE IS A FUTURE,

& YOUR HOPE WILL NOT BE CUT OFF.

-Proverbs 23:18 ESV

{ I DISCOVERED
SOMETHING
ABOUT MYSELF }

Leighann learned a lot about herself through her husband's addiction. Typically she is a rescuer and has the need to be a "fixer." God led her to the revelation that only He is the true Rescuer and Redeemer, not only for her husband, but for her too.

DEAR WOMAN,

I'm no stranger to hurt. I've been betrayed and deceived in ways that people couldn't imagine. I have learned the art (and choice) of forgiveness well. I am thankful for that. I am also thankful that each hurt, each trial, each seemingly setback in my life has served a purpose. I know God has made sure of that. Sometimes you just have to look at things and say, "Maybe this is what it took..." to change you, someone you love, a path you were on, or the way you view things. Whatever it is, it will lead to something better.

Dealing with sexual sin and sexual addiction in a marriage can, quite honestly, take over your whole life if you allow it. As a woman who has been there, I encourage you not to be consumed. I discovered something about myself through this experience that was the beginning of a very long journey of personal growth for me. I am a rescuer, a co-dependent. I learned this behavior early on in life. I would guess that if you are reading this, it's a fair possibility that you can identify with that as well. The lesson (and the good news) in it is this—this is a time of growth for you. Rather than focusing on the needs of your spouse or significant other, this is the time to focus on your own needs. In this situation, the only thing we can control as spouses is ourselves. As frustrating as that can be when you just want it all to stop, you can find some comfort in knowing that focusing on yourself will improve your situation, regardless of your partner's personal choices.

Over the years I have discovered for myself that If I go into a situation planning to "fix it all," I only end up policing and I had my heart broken time and time again. I learned instead to be aware, pray, set boundaries, and require accountability, but not to be the accountability. It only hurt me more and discouraged my partner from truly being honest for fear of causing more hurt.

It takes time to recover, to grow, to get okay; you should be gentle with yourself. For me, I know that as deep and wide as my heart is, in the very depths I felt complete agony. I felt sorrow for what was lost and what I knew would never be the same. But I moved forward and pressed on knowing that the deeper the valleys I faced, the higher the peaks I would climb. I was just passing through. So, I held onto the hand of my Savior determined to press on toward that mark, looking forward to the growth I could expect that can only come from that kind of pain. And it did come, through counseling, through our new church home, and through the wonderful people God brought into our lives. He has directed me, guided me, supported me, and given me a calling to minister to others through all that I've experienced.

Today, I can say, as imperfect as I am, in my weakness He is made strong (2 Corinthians 12:9). I believe in the power of forgiveness and hope. I trust in my Lord to do what is best, knowing that He promises in His Word that He has a plan for me, to give me a hope and a future (Jeremiah 29:11). My life is marked forever by His grace, and I learn more and more each day about walking in it and trusting in what God can do through me rather than what I can do for Him.

LOVE,
LEIGHANN

THE HOPE OF THE RIGHTEOUS BRINGS JOY,

BUT THE EXPECTATION OF THE WICKED WILL PERISH.

-Proverbs 10:28 ESV

THERE IS
'THE OTHER
SIDE'
OF THIS
CHASM

Not all marriages make it. No one goes into marriage thinking theirs will end in divorce. So when you've done all you can to save your marriage and yet you can't control the choices of your spouse, it can be devastating—but it doesn't have to stay that way. Anne knows this all too well after giving herself faithfully to almost two decades of marriage only to have it end by her husband's choice to be with another woman. Anne pressed into the HOPE that God still had a plan for her life—and wow did he ever!

DEAR FRIEND,

It makes me weep to even think of writing this letter to you. I am sorry for your pain. I struggle to force myself to look back on those dark days, to remember what helped me and what didn't. But perhaps that is the key to extending hope to you; that those days are in the past and life is good again.

So, this *can* be my offering of hope to you: that there is "the other side" of this chasm. You *can* cross over to a place of safety, peace, and confidence again. You *can* have your heart and mind shielded from the crippling bitterness. You *can* find happiness again. Your life will never be the same, but isn't something real and true better than living a lie with a partner who is only partially yours? Part of him lives for feeding his addiction and part of him is occupied with covering it up. How much of him is there for you?

Experiencing such perspective-warping betrayal from a man who had been my best friend for many years has been the worst thing I have lived through yet (emphasis on "lived through")! I turned 50 and found myself in the midst of a divorce. I was careful not to trash him to anyone (I didn't want that on my conscience), but I was truthful. And without me around to be the "diplomatic one," I could no longer shield our (adult) kids, family, and friends from his bizarre attitudes and actions. He seemed to really go off the deep end once he was "free of me." For a while, they didn't really know what to believe—or whom. It needles me that so many people believed lies about me, but I've had to continue to reorient to what is most important. People who really know me, know what is true. People who only know me by reputation, well, how much do they really matter?

Please know that I would always encourage everyone to do their best to save their marriage. In my situation, the last three years of our marriage was a time of coming to face the reality that I was the only one married in our relationship. He told me he loved me and would stop seeing other women, but instead, it escalated. By the time I moved out, he was living as if he were single and dating—spending his time, emotional and physical attention as well as our money, on other women.

I hope you will not be faced with divorce. But if you do find yourself coming to that conclusion, I don't see that anyone can tell you how you should go about it. Some people have shown me disdain for hanging in there as long as I did, while others have shown disapproval that I am divorced at all. But this you DO need—true friends. Mature, reliable people who love you (and preferably love your husband too) and who will most certainly keep things confidential! How we need others to help us sort through our thoughts and choices when our emotions are swirling around every-which-way. And if no friends fit that criteria, I would find a professional counselor or pastoral counselor.

So here are the life-preserving things that helped me—things I wish I would have done differently:

• If I had a do-over, I would have been more determined to find someone sooner to confide in. The few I tried to rely on were ill-equipped to be of help, so I gave up. I did not really open up to anyone fully until we had split up. Who knows if it may have saved our relationship to have been in counseling with someone early on?

- I am very grateful for friends who were able to show compassion, but also able to remind me that the marriage had not been *all* bad. No matter how angry I was, they were able to refrain from jumping in on an ex-husband bashing session. I really didn't need their bad feelings added to my own!

- Along those lines, I was also careful how much I vented with family. I knew I would eventually heal because I was aggressively seeking to forgive and shield myself from bitterness. But I knew that with some of my family, that would not be the case. Bitterness is an ugly thing and spreads like a horribly contagious disease!

- I kept in mind that whatever I said to other people could potentially be used against me or put my friends or family in a difficult situation if the divorce could not be settled out of court.

- Although I did need to make new friends and find new interests, I took a few missteps. Fortunately, my best girlfriend was faithful to ask hard questions and greatly helped me from getting in too deep with anyone who was not good for me.

- I did my best not to expect too much from my grown children. I realized very quickly that they were not going to be (nor should they be!) my buddies who I could hang out with (or hang onto) as my sole emotional support. Ultimately, it would push them away if I were too clingy.

- I tried not to console myself with things that would only make more problems. Long-term comfort would not be found in a bottle of fine wine or carafe of martinis. It would not be found in creamy Fettuccine Alfredo or gallons of Blue Bunny ice cream. It would not help to spend my lonely Saturdays shopping either. I was imperfect in all this, but I did go on very long walks (instead of spending money on a gym membership), long drives in my car and limited my shopping to garage sales and flea markets. "How much can I buy for $10?" was my mantra.

- I groped to find my way. Looking back, even though I was 50 yrs old, I unconsciously reverted to styles of dress, hair style, and even demeanor, that were more like what I had been when I met my husband. I found myself an odd conglomeration of who I had been, who I was, and who I was yet to be! I suppose my "look" was updated enough, but again, my best girlfriend (someone I had history with) was such a lifeline to me. Her pointed questions helped keep me from flying too far off the mark of who I really was.

One last thing, I cannot close without telling you that I am whole and happy today because of all the things I listed above. But **the** reason they were doable was not because I was so strong or mature. It was because I sought God in the midst of all that trauma and heartache and He was so ready to help. My best girlfriend was instrumental in my life. She directed me to an excellent Bible study and I made myself go to church. Even when I desperately just wanted to stay home and nurse my wounds or go out and get myself into trouble. I found strength in God and the people He led me to for help. I am absolutely certain that I would be a huge mess if I had allowed my pain and rage to take me away from God instead of toward Him.

I write this letter prayerfully, so if you are reading it—you have been prayed for! May you find in God through His Son, Jesus, all you could ever hope for!

LOVE,
ANNE

"THE LORD IS MY PORTION," SAYS MY SOUL, "THEREFORE I WILL HOPE IN HIM."

-Lamentations 3:24 ESV

{ FEEL ALL THE
FEELINGS,
BUT DON'T
LET THEM
RULE
OVER YOU }

After 25 years of marriage, Kim was awakened to the truth of her imperfect marriage. She found wholeness and healing through dealing with her own false beliefs and unhealthy patterns. Today, both she and her marriage are thriving better than she ever could have imagined.

DEAR FRIEND,

I've a long-held saying, "God uses everything to transform us, even the manure of life." If you've ever had a compost pile, you know the importance of all that refuse forming something rich (even though it can be seen by some people as a steaming pile of stench).

I never expected to have so much crap to add to my life's mulch pile. Not until I learned of my husband's porn addiction (after 25 years of marriage). That sparked an unearthing of my own rubbish, false beliefs, and unhealthy patterns. I wasn't sure our marriage would survive and my life really stunk for that first year or two. Working with a counselor for a couple of years was a key to my personal healing and freedom to be my true self. The three most important aspects of my healing journey were: counseling (individual and marital), one or two trusted safe friends who knew my story and a support group of women who've experienced relational betrayal.

What you're experiencing right now is beyond painful and harder than you never imagined. These are the things I learned early on and the best advice I can offer:

You're not crazy (despite what your feelings are telling you).

You didn't make your man choose to do the things he's done. It's not your fault.

This is hard.

It's okay to be angry.

Feel all the feelings, but don't let them rule over you.

If you're shut down, like I was, discover those feelings and learn how to express them.

Pursue your own recovery and leave your man's recovery up to him.

Let go of any control you thought you had.

This is a season and it will pass. Eventually.

Cling to God. He's the only one who promised to never leave you or betray you.

If your man is honest and willing to pursue his own recovery, your relationship has a chance to truly thrive like never before. I know because mine is more alive and real seven years later than I ever hoped it could be.

You're not alone. Find support and safe people to walk with you through this journey.

**I'M PRAYING FOR YOU TO FIND
YOUR WAY TO WHOLENESS,
KIM**

BEHOLD, THE
EYE OF THE
LORD IS ON
THOSE WHO
FEAR HIM,

ON THOSE
WHO HOPE
IN HIS
STEADFAST
LOVE.

-Psalm 33:18 ESV

{ THIS HAS BEEN A JOURNEY OF DISCOVERY & HEALING }

Oftentimes it is easier to look the other way than to face the reality that there is something going on that can or will detour our agendas, schedules, and hopes and dreams for our lives. So for five years, Susan just told herself that she was going to believe whatever her husband told her was the truth about dealing with his porn problem. However, those five years came to an abrupt end when she had a sudden revelation.

DEAR READER,

On March 19, 2015 the Lord woke me up at 6:18 a.m. and I knew something wasn't right. Once again my husband (not a morning person) was already up and in the den, which had become a habit. I sneaked in and when he saw me, he quickly tried to shut the site down he was looking at, but he knew he was caught. My world proceeded to crumble in front of me. I had caught him looking at porn on TV five years earlier. He said he'd get help, but he didn't. He said it was occasional, mostly a couple of times a year when I was gone out of town on business. We didn't know where to get help and he would get defensive if I asked him how he was doing, then he'd just lie and say "pretty good." So after a while we didn't discuss it anymore.

That morning, I told my husband, through my tears, that I was a strong person and somehow I'd get through this, but I didn't know if that was going to include him or not. He finally understood the gravity of the problem, even though he'd felt out of control for months. I knew I was not going to allow myself to be dishonored and devalued like this anymore. I felt disgusted, shocked, betrayed by my closest friend, dishonored, stupid for believing his lies again, angry, inadequate as a wife, and like I didn't even know this person I'd been married to for almost 37 years. He had worked hard to keep his ugly secret hidden for over 14 years. (By the way, my husband is a pastor, although not currently working as such.)

The next day, a young man my husband had almost "un-followed" on Facebook, posted an article from XXXchurch. com. He looked up the website and began to get help. This was a good sign to me that he took the initiative to start seeking help without my demanding it. He enrolled in a 30-day workshop and got the X3watch software for all our devices (after the 30-day workshop, he joined one of the XXXchurch small groups online). About the third day in, God gave me the grace to see my husband as His broken child. The Lord showed me that there was enough good in my husband worth rescuing. He reminded me that all sin, even mine, is exactly why Jesus had to die for us. None of us deserve His grace. By God's miraculous grace I told him I forgave him, but we still had a long, hard, painful road ahead of us. Since I was seeing him take real steps he'd never taken before to change, I committed to stay and try to work things out.

This last year and a half has been the hardest of my life. I have suffered PTSD symptoms, having moments where it was all I could do to breathe, feeling like an elephant was sitting on my chest. I have a home business and nearly lost it as a result of not being able to care about or concentrate on anything else. I would have a meltdown if a beautiful woman walked past us or was on TV. I was a mess. I did not share "the secret" with anyone because I felt this was my husband's decision if and when to tell. About six months into this journey, my husband realized I did need to talk with someone, so I shared with a close friend who had dealt with this issue, but that had ended in divorce. I decided I needed to see a counselor. I had been focused on helping my husband with his issues, but I realized I needed to take care of myself, too. Eventually we went to counseling together.

This has been a journey of discovery and healing. God is truth, so our "new normal" is to be completely honest with each other.

We began by reading every book and article together, watching every video we could find, and then discussing them. We both have learned multitudes about ourselves, God, this dark addiction, our humanity, and real intimacy. As we learned and talked, I would learn more hurtful things and then have to process them, but God is faithful and loves Truth. We also learned, in a more real way than ever, that we have an enemy, the father of lies, who wants to destroy us. My husband began to learn why he was using porn as his medication. Now we are actually sharing more intimacy than we ever have our whole marriage. God is also helping me in my weak areas. God has used music a lot to minister to us. One song I had never heard before was "Broken Together" by Casting Crowns. I heard it every time I got in the car for a while and it gave me hope. I have also kept a journal of scripture verses that spoke to me that I could read over often.

The journey is not over, but we have both come such a long way. My husband has been free for a year and a half and is successfully dealing with daily temptations. I still have struggles with trust, but much less than at first. For the first time in our marriage, we have real intimacy that my husband was emotionally unable to give me before. Now we want to help others fight this battle and win!

SUSAN

YOU ARE MY HIDING PLACE & MY SHIELD; I HOPE IN YOUR WORD.

-Psalm 119:114 ESV

{ THIS WAS A BROKENNESS I KNEW I WOULD BE ABLE TO HEAL FROM }

Through my work in women's ministry, I've met many women (young and old) who find out about their boyfriends or fiancee's addictions prior to marriage. Carole was one of them. Thankfully Carole listened to her gut and to those who were in her sphere of influence and did what was best for herself this side of marriage. Although she was planning a wedding and was devastated by the idea of calling it off, ultimately she did. And even though it was painful and embarrassing, she survived it and is now able to share her story with others.

DEAR FRIEND,

First, I just want to say that you are not alone even though you may feel desperately alone right now. I know I did. I remember the very moment when I first discovered my fiancé's addiction to pornography. I was shocked, heartbroken, in a state of disbelief and quite honestly, scared. It frightened me that this man, with whom I was planning a wedding, had this very secret, compartmentalized side to his nature. I did not understand how anyone could live a double life like that. Everything else about him seemed so perfect. He was handsome, charming, successful, kind, and he was a Christian! How could this be happening? He was out of town when I stumbled upon the first red flag and I was devastated. I felt like I had been kicked in the stomach. I remember asking people that I knew, hypothetically, if their husbands or significant others looked at pornography and how did that make them feel? Most people just told me to ignore it, that this is just something all men do. A part of me wanted to believe them, and yet my gut told me that it was much deeper than that. I was just beginning my walk with the Lord at that time. I was absolutely a "baby Christian." I thought I was very open-minded and that I could handle it. See, he was the first man in my entire life who told me he wanted to wait until after we were married to have sex. No man in all 43 years of my life ever loved me enough to want to wait. So, this man surely was sent to me from God. I just knew this! To say I was heartbroken is an understatement.

As time went on, I discovered more pornography and the topics of what he was watching became more deviant. I would imagine in my mind that once we were married, I could do some of those things with him and he wouldn't need to seek that out on the internet any longer. I was so afraid of the thought of losing him and often wished I had not found out until after we were already married. Then I would not have to make a tough decision that I knew would lead to my heart being broken. So, I became very sick in my mind and started searching for "evidence." I would search on his computer, through his trash, through his receipts, file cabinets, etc. I found myself doing things I would never do in someone else's home. I was invading his privacy and that was so out of character for me. The more I searched and found, the more he would become angry and blame me, telling me that I was just paranoid.

There is a often a pattern in an addict's behavior, where they cannot accept responsibility for their own actions, so they constantly blame others. I was so caught up in the lies that I started to blame myself. As women, we are bombarded with these unattainable and unrealistic standards of how we should look and being in love with this man, with this horrible addiction, just exacerbated my insecurities. I was constantly aware of him looking at others, wondering if he was lusting after them or comparing me with them.

He was Catholic and the Lord saved me in that church, which was also where we were going to get married. After my discovery, he agreed to meet with our priest for counseling. I thought that was the answer! The priest had nothing to offer us, except a few words to me, that perhaps I should wait to marry this man. After that, I would sit in church week after week and wonder how many other women were crying and screaming inside, full of pain and yet no one talked about it.

Gratefully at the time, the Lord led me to an online Christian support group that was facilitated then by the director of

Recover.org. Oh my goodness, suddenly I was no longer alone in this nightmare! I found support, love, encouragement, and ladies who could all truly relate and understand exactly how I was feeling. It did not take the pain away, but I had an outlet, the Lord gave me some of my dearest Christian sisters and it was truly my lifeline. Through that forum, I began to learn how to develop a personal relationship with God and I began to rely on Him more and more. To be able to share me and my fiances deepest, darkest secrets with these ladies, knowing that it would go nowhere, was lifesaving. This addiction is not one we can just share with anyone. It's not as socially acceptable as other addictions. In my situation, the man that I was engaged to had an upper level management position, so even as angry and hurt as I was, I could not and would not divulge his secret and damage his reputation or career.

We went on for several years and he would try recovery of different types, but never stuck with them. I had such high hopes for us and I believed that he would recover, we would have this miraculous testimony to share as a married couple. We would be able to offer hope to other couples down the road! I believed that for several years with all my heart. However, that never happened. I finally ended the relationship once and for all, once the pain of staying with him became unbearable. My hopes and dreams of being married to him were shattered. Yes, I was completely broken, but this was a brokenness I knew I would be able to heal from, with the help of God and my precious sisters in Christ. Now, looking back many years later, I'm so grateful that God provided me with the knowledge and strength to walk away. I have so much to be thankful for!

Perhaps your engagement or your marriage is one that will survive this and I know that is possible and I pray that for you! I've seen it happen! I also want you to know that if it does not, there is peace and joy to be found again. I want you to know right now that no matter how you feel, you are not alone. This addiction he has is not about you. You could be a supermodel and it would not change his behavior. I can promise you that. We tend to think that if only we were different in some way— taller, blonder, slimmer, younger, and the list is endless—then he would love us and not need to seek his fulfillment else-where. That is a lie. Please know that. You are loved. You are enough. Most importantly, YOU ARE BEAUTIFUL. This addiction steals so much from us, but there is healing. There truly is hope on the other side.

I am praying for you, beautiful friend.

LOVE IN HIM,
CAROLE

BLESSED IS HE WHOSE HELP IS THE GOD OF JACOB,

WHOSE
HOPE IS
IN THE
LORD
HIS GOD.

-Psalm 146:5 ESV

{ GOD DOES NOT SEE YOU AS YOUR HUSBAND SEEMS TO SEE YOU }

Through Rebecca's journey, she learned that the most important eyes for her were God's. She learned in the midst of trials and setbacks what her true value and worth were measured by: Her Creator's endless love and pursuit of healing for her heart. She learned much about scripture and God's promises while seeking Him during the hurdles in her marriage.

DEAR WOMAN,

You are most likely reading this because you are in deep pain due to your husband's sexual addiction. Please let me share with you some things God has taught me in my own journey through my husband's addiction. I hope and pray that they may encourage and bless you.

God does not see you as your husband seems to see you. Psalms 139:14 states that you are wonderfully and beautifully made, while Proverbs 18:22 says that a man who finds a wife finds a good thing and obtains favor from the Lord. God says you are a blessing and a wonderful gift, but unfortunately your husband probably won't see this through his sin and addiction-tainted eyes.

God loves you dearly. The Bible has much to say about your worth in Christ, too much to place in this letter. I encourage you to study scripture in seeking your worth as God's child. Here you will find strength, peace, and joy.

I have also learned sexual addiction doesn't just lie to those trapped in it, but also to those who care about the addict. Personally, it made me feel completely worthless, ugly, and dirty. But I learned that my husband's addiction and choices reflect who he is, not who I am; this truth is the same for you. Your husband's sexual addiction and choices reflect who he is, not who you are. You are enough, you are precious, and you are lovable. Beauty is in the eye of the beholder and as God's daughter, He beholds you. He determines your worth and value, not your husband.

Another thing I wish to share with you that God has graciously taught me is that He wants us to come to Him boldly (humbly, yet boldly). Old Testament prophets prayed this way and Jesus encourages it in the New Testament. We are God's children, and we can freely approach Him. God is approachable! We are never a bother to God; He wants us to come to Him freely.

Prayer is also an action, God uses it as a means to an end and it also teaches and blesses us. Don't grow weary praying for your husband. He heals the brokenhearted and binds up their wounds. (Psalms 147:3)

**MAY THE LORD RICHLY BLESS
YOU AND YOUR MARRIAGE.
REBECCA**

FOR

THROUGH

THE SPIRIT,

BY FAITH,

WE
OURSELVES
EAGERLY
WAIT FOR
THE HOPE OF
RIGHTEOUSNESS.

-Galatians 5:5 ESV

> {
> **I AM THE**
> **DAUGHTER**
> **OF THE MOST**
> **HIGH & DESERVE**
> **TO BE TREATED**
> **AS SUCH**
> }

Many wives have wondered if they should partake of watching porn, making home movies, taking nude selfies (or even more) to satisfy their husband's desires. I've heard women say more times than I can count: "If he is going to watch it, I'd rather him watch it with me than without me." Christina learned the hard way that taking that path often leads to getting burned. She writes transparently from her experience.

DEAR FRIEND,

Please know you're not alone in what feels like an empty, dark, and hopeless place in realizing your marriage has been tainted with sexual immorality. I myself fell into this pit and deep down inside I knew better than to entertain my ex-husband's sexual fantasies. But, I thought our love and marriage were solid enough to dabble. We were very wealthy, were in good physical shape, and were caught up in the wealth and pop culture. We thought we could play with fire and not get burned. I don't have to go into detail, but I think you know by my context clue (ex-husband), that we were wrong.

If I had to do it all over again, of course, I would have put my foot down and stuck to my moral upbringing, but I have learned God is in control of all things, good, and bad. "Would of, could of, should of..." is a waste of time. During my divorce, I spent a lot of time running to Jesus for forgiveness, which I received. I also asked for forgiveness from another couple we were involved with, which was a really hard and an awkward thing to do, but I know God wanted me to do this. Once the dust settled and my divorce was a reality, I begged God to cleanse the memories of my sexual immorality and if He was ever to give me another husband, I didn't care what he had or didn't have as long as he was a Godly man and in love with Jesus!

I am using this experience to understand what I was never taught as a young girl. I am learning about God's design for marriage. God wants us to wait and pray for our future husbands and current husbands. I also learned that I am a daughter of the Most High and deserve to be treated as such. I really didn't know what love was or how to recognize it. I am learning how to love and be loved by God's standards now and not by the world's.

I know this feels overwhelming, but take a deep breath and take it day by day, God will carry you through. He hears all your prayers and is bottling up every single one of your tears. He loves you so much. Please learn about His love for you and let him put those shattered pieces of your heart back together, seared with His promises, love, and wisdom. Perhaps God is going to make the man you have now all you deserve and heal your marriage. Or perhaps He will heal your broken heart and give you the Godly man you desire and deserve some day. Trust Him with all your heart. I am a true testimony of God's restoration. God is so loving my friend, just lay all you're going through at His feet and let Jesus heal your heart. God is jealous for your beautiful broken heart and wants to give you all you deserve, but mostly Jesus wants your heart first.

**WITH LOVE,
CHRISTINA**

REMEMBER YOUR WORD TO YOUR SERVANT,

IN WHICH
YOU HAVE
MADE
ME HOPE.

-Psalm 119:49 ESV

{ I AM
BETTER
OFF
NOW }

Jill placed expectations on her husband that she never should have, but that didn't mean he was justified in his seeking sexual gratification elsewhere. Jill was crazy about God while her husband was crazy about porn. Their marriage did not survive, but Jill did and, although it was hell going through it, she says she is better off now because of it.

DEAR CRUSHED WOMAN,

I grew up the only child to parents who didn't express their love very well. They also had a tendency to call me names that were character attacking and caused me to struggle with low self-esteem. I never knew how much God loved me or that my value should come from Him.

At 15, I did what an unloved girl would do: I met a boy and did things I shouldn't have. At 17, I met the man I would eventually marry two years later at the young age of 19. I placed expectations on my husband that I shouldn't have. I thought he would be my "knight in shining armor" and I would forever be loved and cherished.

Those dreams were shattered when I found out about his porn use. He brought magazines into our marriage and that was enough to keep him from me. And then when the internet was invented—well, you know how it is. My self-esteem was shattered worse than ever before. I wondered how could the man who had vowed to love me forever allow this to come in between us?

It turns out that that he continued with his porn use our entire marriage. Even the five years that I thought he was doing well, he was lying to my face. My mistake was allowing my identity to be twisted with what he did or said.

It wasn't until a man explained sexual addiction to me that I started to grasp the truth. Once I realized this was HIS problem and had nothing to do with me, I started down a healing path.

Finding online support ministries were helpful as well. Just knowing that I wasn't alone made a huge difference for me.

I went through a huge process with God. I finally found my identity in Him. I realized that no matter what my husband said or did, I was dearly loved by my Heavenly Father and that helped me get through the rough times.

One evening in August of 2012, my husband told me that he didn't love me anymore and that I was too Godly. This was just a couple of months before our 19th wedding anniversary.

I was devastated. I felt like I was living for God, doing all that He had called me to do and now had received the ultimate slap in the face.

My heart hurt for months as he decided to leave, then changed his mind. We went to counseling, but he wasn't really trying. He was mean to me most of those times, up until he finally left in March of 2013.

I am better off now. I am fully living for the Lord. I work at a church, I am in leadership at the church I attend, and nothing is stopping me from living the way I know God has called me to.

Raising three teenagers without my ex-husband's emotional support has proved challenging, but I have family and friends who are praying with and for me.

Divorce doesn't define me. My value and self-worth come from my Heavenly Father, who says I'm His masterpiece created for good works. So are you!

Allow God to revive your spirit. He promises to bind up the brokenhearted and heal their wounds. Thankfully, He ALWAYS keeps His promises.

GOD BLESS YOU,
JILL

AS IT IS MY
EAGER
EXPECTATION
& HOPE THAT
I WILL NOT
BE AT ALL
ASHAMED,

BUT THAT WITH FULL COURAGE NOW AS ALWAYS CHRIST WILL BE HONORED IN MY BODY, WHETHER BY LIFE OR BY DEATH.

-Philippians 1:20 ESV

**ALL I
WANTED TO
DO WAS
SOLVE THE
PROBLEM**

Like many of us, Jennifer wanted to control her husband's addiction. Through much perseverance, she learned that the easiest way to fix her husband's addiction was to surrender it to God. Listen to her share two powerful truths that can speak to us all.

HI FRIEND,

I want you to know two things above all else:

1. This is not your fault.
Your husband, or boyfriend, or fiancé is not struggling with porn or _____ because you are not measuring up, or because you're not pretty enough, or because you're not performing well enough.

2. This is not your problem to solve.
I wish I could have understood this truth when my husband and I were in the beginning stages of overcoming his porn addiction. All I wanted to do was solve the problem, fix it, make it go away. But I realized, in the hardest way, that it was something that was totally out of my control. It was an addiction that I could not talk him out of or make him feel guilty about. It was something that he had to deal with on his own, with the guidance of the Holy Spirit. I realized that the best thing I could do to "fix" the problem was completely surrender it all to God. After all, He's the Great Physician. He's the only one who can break chains that grip so tightly to the heart and mind of our husbands.

I always want to sugar-coat the healing process when I talk to other wives about it. I want to say that, once he realizes it's an addiction, he suddenly stops watching porn, stops the affairs, stops the lingering glances at women in the store—but it doesn't happen that way. It is a bumpy, painful, and very long road, oftentimes showered with relapses and falls. But in the end, recovery is possible for your husband. Healing is possible for you.

Have hope that there is a light at the end of the tunnel of addiction. I have been in that place where I swore there would never be an end, that there was no light. I have been in that place where I saw the light and then watched it fade away. But I have also been at that place when I saw the light and I breathed the fresh air that was waiting for me at the other end of that long tunnel.

HAVE HOPE IN CHRIST'S POWER, FRIEND.
JENNIFER

BUT CHRIST
IS FAITHFUL
OVER GOD'S
HOUSE
AS A SON.

& WE ARE
HIS HOUSE
IF INDEED WE
HOLD FAST
OUR CONFIDENCE
& OUR BOASTING
IN OUR HOPE.

-Hebrews 3:6 ESV

{
I GOT
SERIOUS
ABOUT
JESUS
}

Ashlee, the wife of a marine, learned about her husband's infidelty through checking his texts and voicemail messages. Devastated to learn that she wasn't the only woman in his life, she was determined to fight for her marriage and not be another divorce statistic of the military. Even when it seemed hopeless, she encouraged herself in the Lord.

SWEET FRIEND,

I know that if you're reading this, then life has most likely taken you on an unintended journey and for that I am sorry. No one wants to go through what people like me have experienced. It's the most gut-wrenching, terrible feeling in the world when the person you love betrays you. I know what it's like to check text messages, voicemails, and emails only to discover that you're not the only woman in your husband's life after he promised that he was telling the truth for the second, fourth, or fifth time.

My husband and I got married when we were both 18. We joined the Marines a few months later and shipped off to boot camp. I don't know how much you know about the military lifestyle, but infidelity and pornography are rampant. The divorce rate in the Marines is off the charts. The odds were completely stacked against us from the beginning and we knew that, but we chose to fight anyway. Or at least I did.

There were so many situations I went through where I would try to seek out advice or guidance that ended up making things worse. I grew up in church and I was brought up with the mentality that, if someone cheated, then the answer was divorce. I kept trying to find someone to tell me what to do if that wasn't what I wanted. Thankfully, I found a strong community of believers who did not judge me and encouraged me to fight for my marriage. Their encouragement increased my faith and gave me the strength I needed to keep fighting.

I clearly remember the day I resolved to fight for my marriage. I was praying out loud in my house when I said, "I'm drawing a line in the sand." Satan had stolen everything from me and I was not about to let him take anymore. He might have taken the purity of my marriage, but he was not going to have my husband without a fight from me. I had to be a warrior woman, put up my dukes and get down to it! When I began to understand that there was a battle waging against my marriage, I got serious about prayer. I got serious about being in the Bible and I got serious about Jesus. When I say serious, don't take that to mean everything was boring, dreary, bleak, or droll. Quite the opposite!

I learned to read and believe scripture. One of my favorite scriptures (I would recite to myself every time I was feeling down) was Joel 2:25. "I will restore to you the years that the swarming locust has eaten, the hopper, the destroyer, and the cutter, my great army, which I sent among you." Believers know that nothing can happen to them outside of God's will or without Him knowing about it. I trusted God when something terrible was happening in my marriage because I knew He promised that He would restore whatever I lost. I knew this didn't mean He was going to necessarily restore my marriage, but that He would restore my life.

My husband and I nearly got divorced. Our relationship faced a lot of uncertainty. One thing that was crucial to my recovery during that time was having safe people in my life. I call them that because I had a lot of friends, but very few of my friends were who I considered safe people. I knew that these few friends were strong believers who cared more about my holiness than happiness, which was very important for me because I needed accountability.

When your relationship is in trouble, it can leave you feeling very vulnerable and desperate. In my experience, vulnerable and desperate leads to destruction and bad decisions. I had two very close friends that I called my Aaron and my Hur (Exodus 17:11-13). Everyone needs an Aaron and a Hur. These two men of the Bible held up Moses' arms when he was too weak to stand anymore to defeat an invading army. Sometimes you will be too weak to stand alone. That's why you need reliable, trustworthy people who will stand with you.

I am happy to tell you that God **did** restore my marriage. I had expectations that once we got back together everything would be perfect and the way it should be, but I was wrong.

There was so much damage and hurt we had to work through. We invested in a good marriage counselor and worked with her every week for six months. We are about to celebrate our tenth wedding anniversary and our second year of recovery together. It is hard work, but it was worth everything we went through to be where we are today. If you had told me two years ago that I would be where I am now, I wouldn't have believed it. What I once hoped for is now my reality. I know I am tremendously blessed to be loved by the God who loved me first.

KEEP THE FAITH,
ASHLEE

AND WE DESIRE

EACH ONE OF

YOU TO SHOW

THE SAME

EARNESTNESS

TO HAVE THE

FULL ASSURANCE

OF HOPE

UNTIL THE END.

-Hebrews 6:11 ESV

{ BEING 'STRONG' IS ASKING FOR GOD'S HELP }

It is understandable that the pain of betrayal can cause us to isolate ourselves and to push away the very peo-ple we love in fear that if we keep them close, they will harm us again. Jessica knows this all too well as she spent years pointing the finger at others for her pain and using it as an excuse to iso-late, grow bitter and negative; while always waiting for the bottom to drop out.

DEAR WOMAN,

Someone once told me, "Dealing with hard circumstances can either make you or break you." And to tell you the truth, dealing with hard circumstances "breaks you" and only if you are willing to face those hard circumstances do they "make you" stronger. Although I do have to admit, I'm a very stubborn person and believe me, its hurt me more than it's helped.

I've been married for seven years and the last six have been full of brokenness, loneliness, and despair. Broken because trust was no longer in existence. I was always on pins and needles thinking it would happen again. During that dark season in my life, I questioned God and my husband, but never did I question myself. I was quick to point the finger at everyone who should've been there to bring comfort and keep my husband accountable. I was quick to blame my husband because he instilled fear and doubt and put us through an almost divorce. I let those emotions fester in me so much so that even when he came clean and asked for forgiveness, I would remind him of what made him fall and how much he had hurt me.

Because I never stopped to look at myself, I had forgotten about God's forgiveness, promises, and love over my life. Negativity consumed me and instead of helping my husband understand my emotional needs, I pushed him away. It was easier for him to revert back to what (he thought) would take him away from the circumstances we were going through. He had multiple affairs because we both just didn't know how to deal with all it. He would run straight to what kept us from facing the problem. I was negative and he was isolating. Both facing nothing, both embracing sin. (This is not to say that your husband's actions are your fault, this is to help understand how to respond in great adversity.)

Now looking back, I missed an amazing opportunity to finally have God all to myself and be completely vulnerable: cry, be angry, sad, question. Instead I moved on and called it being "strong." I told myself, "I'm a big girl and big girls don't show weakness, they move on." The world says being "strong" is not allowing bad experiences to happen twice because after once, you should be prepared. You should become "stronger" because of those experiences. I learned that being "strong" is asking for God's help and asking for help from those who have lived the same experience, in return you begin the start of the healing process. To be "strong" is not giving in to what the world expects of you, but what God delights in; love, for-giveness, faith, hope, mercy, grace, etc.

Loneliness can also be so paralyzing in your healing process. You may feel embarrassed to share, manipulated because of reputation, or simply think you're going through this alone. Know God is picking up the pieces even when we don't see it. He sees the beauty in our brokenness, and even through the heartache and turmoil, God still sees the worth and beauty in you.

Going through something like this is never easy, but I promise you this too shall pass and you will see freedom take place in you if you let it. Trust the process God allows. It's hard to imagine love and happiness after a storm. But after the storm comes peace. The peace God gave us was more than enough to get us through it. The love we once felt for each other has multiplied to more than what I'd imagined possible. It's become easier to open up to others and help those that are going through it because we both decided to talk things through and get out of that darkness together. We found that helping others through our experience brought us closer to each other and to God, with love and peace that surpasses all understanding.

SINCERELY,
JESSICA

I WILL RETURN
HER VINEYARDS
TO HER &
TRANSFORM
THE VALLEY OF
TROUBLE
INTO A GATEWAY
OF HOPE.

- Hosea 2:15 NLT

{
I LET HIS
ADDICTION
DICTATE
MY LIFE
}

We women often think we know what we're getting into when a discovery or revelation is made about our relationship. We choose to move forward thinking it is one thing, only to find out after the fact, it is another. This was the case with Dawn, who found out that trying to carry the addiction of another person will weigh you down until you can no longer stand on your own.

DEAR FRIEND,

Many people thought I was crazy for marrying a man with a pornography addiction and honestly I wondered for many years why I did. My response to them was, "At least I knew what I was getting into." Truth is, I had no idea what kind of battle I was up against. I knew that I was marrying a man who loved God with all his might. I knew that I was marrying a man who would go to the grave for me. But for a long time I was hurting. At times I couldn't see past his struggle.

In the very beginning of our marriage, he asked me to be his support, to pray him through and of course, I did. He would confide in me and tell me he was struggling and I would put on a brave face—a positive attitude—and become his armor bearer. I would tell him I loved him and would pray right there for him. While outwardly I was this brave wife, inwardly I would cry out to God and ask him to stand in the gap for my heart.

I asked God to show me when he was struggling and many times He did, but I also asked God to protect my heart. I would ask my husband how he was doing and every time he would come out and tell me what was going on. I would then go through a struggle of my own. I wondered if I was good enough, pretty enough. I wondered if I satisfied him in the way that he needed. After awhile I started to spiral and his addiction consumed me. I would wonder all the time if he was being honest with me, if he was sleeping around with other women and even if he paid for sex. I let his addiction dictate my life. I let it tell me how I should dress, look, and be. I was so lost that I didn't see what was right up the road.

One day God told me to take my focus off my husband's addiction and place it on God. He spoke to my heart and told me the truth. He showed me that I was precious and beautiful. God restored my identity. He reminded me that, no matter where my husband was in his addiction, I was His daughter, a true princess. I finally gave God my husband's addiction. I let it go and have been freed from a bondage I didn't even realize I was trapped in. God gave me hope during that dark time. Shortly after that my husband was set free! He has been walking in complete freedom and purity, it has changed the way he lives and the way he loves. I always knew he loved me, but now I know and see that he loves me in a way that only God could show him.

My life has been completely transformed, but it wasn't until I let God handle my husband and allowed Him to reveal my heart to me. There is freedom and liberty in allowing Christ to take control. My prayer for you is that God reveals to you your true identity. Who He has made you to be. You are more than this addiction.

**RESPECTFULLY,
DAWN**

WHY, MY SOUL, ARE YOU DOWNCAST? WHY SO DISTURBED WITHIN ME?

PUT YOUR HOPE IN GOD, FOR I WILL YET PRAISE HIM, MY SAVIOR & MY GOD.

-Psalm 42:11 NIV

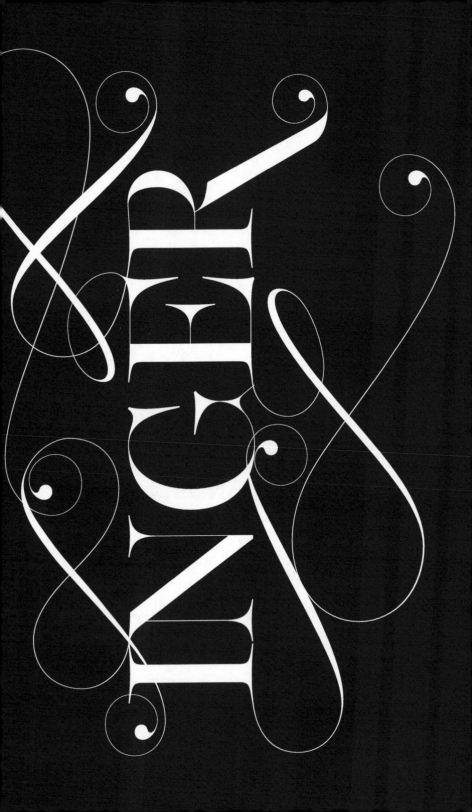

{ CHECK YOUR HEART }

Walking the road of suffering has the potential to awaken us to new understandings about God, ourselves, others, and about life in general. Inger writes about four understandings that took her off guard, but changed her perspective and gave her what she needed to heal from the wounds of many forms of sexual betrayal.

DEAR EXHAUSTED ONE,

In considering writing a letter to you, I was compelled to write regarding four understandings that surprised me along the journey my husband and I have taken:

One: I come from childhood sexual abuse and had always assumed that I was broken and slanted when it came to porn. Porn is what influenced the person to molest my five-year-old person. Once I found a sisterhood of women to journey with and was no longer silent and alone in any of my journey, I was most shocked to discover that women with NO sexual abuse were also just as hurt by their husband's porn usage. The lying by omission and all of it. My hurt was beyond the childhood hurt. Others with all sorts of backgrounds felt the same hurt.

Two: Looking back and walking beside others has shown me that it is extremely important to follow the Spirit and to encourage others to do the same. Seek and follow the Spirit's leading because He knows your story, your husband's story, and what makes each of you do what you do. He knows every hair on your head. It might seem strange at times to follow a leading that is opposite of popular Christian-ese, but the Lord cannot be put in a box. And His Word is so much deeper than quick and popular quotes from the Bible. And none of our stories, personalities, or temperaments are one-size-fits-all. He truly loves everyone involved in your household. He truly wants you to lean into Him and others, and be willing to tackle this issue and get real about it. Encourage each other to seek the Spirit and follow the Spirit. Don't make my mistake and become so enamored with some result and then speak as if this is the answer for all. Share your journey in 'I' statements and let the Spirit highlight in other sisters' journeys what they need.

Three: Don't approach anything the Spirit leads you to as THE answer that will change your husband. God is loving and will ask of you to partner with Him in trying to awaken your husband's soul, but He also leaves him with a free will. Nothing in the journey is a guarantee to work. The Lord wants you to grow in Him and wishes the same thing for your spouse, but each person separately has to be a willing participant with God to grow and make changes.

Four: Check your heart, check your heart, check your heart! The Father makes it clear in Scripture that He measures and looks at our hearts. If your heart is coming from a vindictive place, He will know. If you make moves or follow through in a punish-and-reward manipulative way, the Lord will know and so will your spouse. Authenticity is a very important place to work from with your spouse and with God.

I know you are most likely tired, near your rope's end and there is very little left on the trust thread of your marriage. Be encouraged: I had one tiny little microscopic thin thread remaining. If that one broke, then there was nothing left. It was at that very point when I was at my most authentic and I broke free from living in fear of abandonment. I am pleased to report we made it and both chose to grow beyond many aspects that needed changing.

The sisters I have made through my journey are still very dear and near to my heart. Some of their marriages made it through and some did not, but each followed the Spirit and each continues to grow in Him and that is a wonderful place to be; no matter the outcome.

MUCH LOVE DEAR SISTER IN CHRIST,
INGER

LET US HOLD UNSWERVINGLY TO THE HOPE WE PROFESS, FOR HE WHO PROMISED IS FAITHFUL.

-*Hebrews 10:23 NIV*

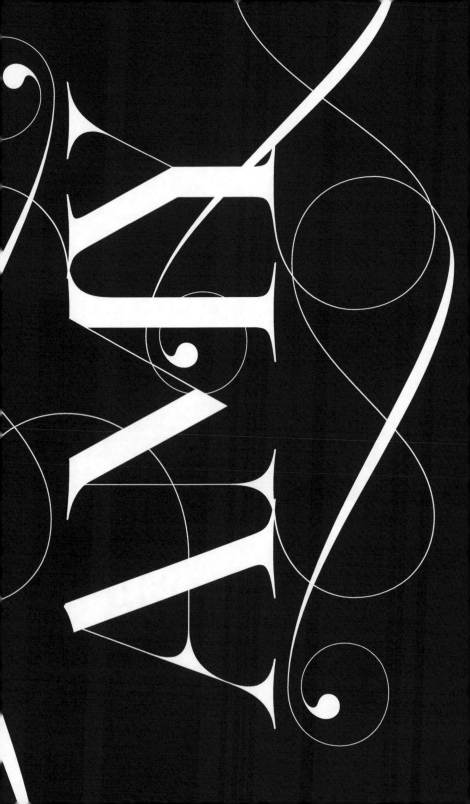

{ LET THIS
EXPERIENCE
BRING
RECLAMATION
& REBIRTH
INTO
YOUR LIFE }

Personally, I believe there is nothing great-er in the midst of hurt and betrayal than to be loved, encouraged, and validated. While at the same time, being gently challenged to pursue healing for yourself. Amy has a beautiful way of acknowledging the pain of others while showing the importance of pursuing their own healing because she's been there herself. She knows what it's like to have the wind knocked out of her, but she also knows what it's like to rise from the rubble better than she was before.

DEAREST SISTER,

I can feel your fractured heart from afar. That feeling you've held in your body for so long that is now confirmed with the discovery of your partner's struggles with sex and pornography addiction. I feel those knots in your stomach, that racing heart, that lump in your throat, that tension in your neck and jaw, and that pressure building in your head. I see your shock, grief, momentary loss of hope, numbness, judgement, and rage. I am here to offer you some hope; to share with you bits of wisdom I have because of living a pain-filled marriage. My heart was full of judgment and closed off to authentic intimacy, while his heart was grieving love lost in so many forms, which eventually led him to using porn to feel safe and loved.

I am here to encourage you to take a deep breath and walk into this shadow; to let this experience bring reclamation and rebirth into your life. What I've learned and keep learning is that when there's no more pretending—the pain cuts deeper. I can offer you encouragement by letting you know that this is "Heaven's knife," as Josh Garrels says. You see, I'm not here to make you feel better, to swoop in and take away your pain. Honestly, one of the hardest things I've discovered through my years of marriage is that pain is our gift and my marriage is my teacher; my husband is my mirror, set to show me the parts of myself I don't want to look at. And if we can have just enough courage to move forward one step at a time and discover what it means to love ourselves, we will heal and become more like the women we were created to be. My hope for you is deep inner transformation and an awakening to who you are as your most authentic self, created in the image of the Divine.

Painfully, yes, these things we feel in our bodies and our hearts are absolutely necessary for healing to begin. This is what took place on the cross of Christ. Despite fear that makes us metaphorically sweat blood, we too must be able to die.

So, no more secrets my darling—for us, for our partner, and for our relationship. Turn and look at the devastated ruins of who we thought we were and the relationship we thought we possessed. We say "I do" at the altar and have a beautiful image of "for better or worse." But did we really know what this would mean? No way. And even if we had some foreshadowing, we didn't really know, because we were yet to experience it with our partner and feel it in our bones. "He who increases knowledge increases suffering." How many of us married as a part of an illusion? I know I did. Hoping that my aches and pains would be healed as I loved my Creator, committed myself to my man and devoted myself to healing the world.

Regardless of whether we stay with our husbands or move on, there are truths to be learned here. What I wish I would've known then is that a part of me prayerfully brought this pain into my life to break my heart open so I could have the suffering I needed to heal my own familiar wounds. This was just a catalyst of sorts. The tip of the iceberg. It's more than just a familial dynamic that drew this partner with this particular pain into my life; it is spiritual and meant for my own redemption. Let your heart burn until you are singing over the real you.

This is painfully beautiful...it's perfect.

For this reason, I do wish I would have judged less—pornography, my husband, and mostly myself. Inevitably, it's acid to wounds and hurts everyone worse. It feels so counterintuitive not to judge a partner's porn and sexual behaviors. I initially believed my husband was disgusting or perverse in some way. I couldn't see that my husband was seeking what every human needs—which is absolute acceptance, deep understanding, and unwavering love. And this is mostly about his relationship with self and only shows up secondarily in his relationship with others.

You may be curious how you can love yourself, be true to yourself, and not feel your emotions and speak your truth. I am in no way suggesting you suppress those parts of yourself. It is helpful to write these things out and share them with a trusted, neutral and non-judgmental friend or professional who will not sway you in a certain direction, unless your safety is at risk. Take some time to scream in your pillow until the screams turn into deep wails. Punch your pillow; kick your feet if you feel the need. Feel everything when you are in a space that is safe to express it and others are safely away. There you can find the truth your spirit has been whispering in your ear. That is the key to your freedom and then you will be ready with clarity and strength to speak your truth and share your needs. This is the space to be in before making big decisions or declarations.

Define honesty differently. Don't torment yourself with the images or all the details. Keep your mind in check as thoughts and pictures come forward. If you can't release what's coming up in a safe space, then tell yourself you will create space for them later. Breathe and nurture the places that ache in your body.

Do request integrity. Integrity is more based on his pilgrimage towards health and healing and not about his daily thoughts and actions or whether or not he is currently medicating with porn or sexual activity. There are signs that demonstrate your partner is moving towards healing with integrity. This is about courage, not perfection.

One more thing: LOVE YOURSELF. Passionately pursue yourself until every cell in your body feels desirable, beautiful, powerful, and sexy to YOU. Do this and one day you will be so connected to yourself that you just might fall head over heels in love with you. From this place every other love that comes your way will just be an overflow.

**ALL MY LOVE AND ABUNDANT
BLESSINGS AS YOU FEEL THE FIRE,
AMY**

BUT IF WE
HOPE FOR
WHAT WE
DO NOT
YET HAVE,

WE WAIT
FOR IT
PATIENTLY.

-*Romans 8:25 NIV*

MICHELLE'S STORY

PART 2

Oh how I hope these letters have been a balm to your soul. And now dear one, there is one letter that remains—the rest of *my* letter to you.

When I started down this road 15 years ago, there was nothing like Recover.org out there. My work with XXXchurch came out of searching for help on the internet for my own marriage. It was the only ministry of its kind that offered an online forum where those who struggled (and their loved ones, too) could come and talk about it and pray for one another. I had no idea then that God would call me to work and serve many through XXXchurch. I am so grateful that he has used the very thing that the enemy tried to destroy me with as a provision and purpose in my life. I am grateful that, out of all of this, you now have a resource to help you through this that many of us never had.

The truth is, prior to this life-changing betrayal, I only *thought* I knew the Lord. I began going to church in my twenties and soon thereafter served as a youth leader, but I never really knew what it was like to depend on God. To make everyday life decisions, truly seeking His direction. I never truly knew the scriptures for myself—only what I heard through attending church services, events, online sermons, or even from the lyrics of popular Christian songs.

But when you have something like this cut you so deep that you are face down in the dust, there are only two choices—stay there or get up. I'll be the first to admit there were times I stayed down. But I am so thankful I had some people in my life who, even though they didn't fully understand all the dynamics of what was going on, pointed me to God's promises for my life. I found hope in those promises. I began to allow God to be the source of my comfort, the source of my healing, and the source of my fulfillment. I sought him out wholly in everything I did for the first time in my life. Slowly I began standing up and living life independently from how my husband was doing on any given day.

Having people who care about you and who can point you to scriptures for hope and encouragement is monumental, but there were things I faced in my journey that I wish someone knew how to help me process. I needed someone to get down in the pit with me on the darkest of days and sojourn alongside, if only to hold my head up in the darkness. I needed unconditional love and acceptance in the times when I responded poorly to my husband's betrayal and relapses due to his sexual sin. There was so much uncertainty as I navigated much of this alone. Some of those things I now have clarity and answers to and want to share them with others.

For example, it is absolutely understandable that dealing with this betrayal in your marriage will make you angry. For some of us who have suffered multiple rejections in life, the feelings of anger are multiplied. I remember moments of great hatred toward my husband for destroying our relationship, our bond, and our love for one another. This was my marriage too, something I wanted, something I valued, and he was stealing it from me. I had no control or say in the matter. I was angry at God. I remember even hearing myself say things aloud directly to God like, "How can a loving and merciful God who knew all that my childhood entailed, all that my life had contained and all of the brokenness—a God who knew my only wish was to have someone in my life who truly loved me and here I am in covenant with someone you knew would destroy me!? How could you allow this man to even come into my life? I feel duped and I feel stuck and I have no idea how this is going to end!"

I wish I had sought good counseling and accountability for myself concerning all of my reactions and responses to this whole thing years before I did. It would have saved us both a lot of heartache. Just because someone hurts us deeply doesn't give us the right to be vengeful or to beat the other person down with our pain. I found myself doing this repeatedly as a defense mechanism. There were times when I would say the most hurtful things to my husband, attacking his character and assaulting his spirit for his double-minded lifestyle that was destroying me.

God had to get hold of my heart and help me in order to restore me to a place of self-control concerning my anger. My anger was justified in many of the situations I faced, but my reactions were out of control. With each incident I grew more hateful toward my husband. I saw his addiction as a choice and something he could control and just stop if he wanted to. The truth is, it *is* a choice to pursue something or to become complacent. Even not choosing to do the right thing is still a choice, but it is so much more complex than that with addictions that have physiological and psychological components to them.

There is a way to break free, but it is not always a 1-2-3, cut-and-dried answer and we tend to forget that addicts become full of despair, anger, fear, and hopelessness. My husband was never in control of his addiction—his addiction was in control of him. Some of the Christian ministries we sought for help believed this to be a lie from the devil and that my husband was choosing to feed his flesh rather than surrender to God. While yes, there is definitely some truth in that, it just wasn't that simple and when I stated this, they said I was in denial, which served to make me further crazy!

Having a compassionate heart towards your spouse is not giving him a hall pass to continue betraying and deceiving you. Having a compassionate heart is more about you and your well-being than it is about him. It is about having the heart of Christ. But, I was so broken for so long that I didn't embrace this healing for quite some time. I held onto the lie that if I offered compassion towards my husband, then I was saying neglect and abuse through his sin in our marriage was okay, which it absolutely was and is not.

I was so confused, so heartbroken, and so disappointed. I wanted more than anything for us to be the couple that defeated sin and had a testimony that would serve multitudes of others. I proclaimed every scripture that said so! I fasted, I prayed, I endured and endured and endured. But the reality was, I wanted it more than my husband wanted it. I could not control his free will, I couldn't force him to deal with what was destroying us and that infuriated me. I was angry with my husband and I was angry with God and I grew tired and bitter.

In our first year of marriage, we left the church we were in for another that my husband said could offer him more accountability. I was sad to leave the people I knew and trusted prior to our marriage, but I was hopeful that if my husband was willing to be open, honest, and walk with others (even if somewhere else), then our marriage could be saved.

I had such high hopes, but they soon faded when those who were supposed to be leading and helping us seemingly saw me as part of the problem. I felt so misunderstood for so long by the very people I should have been able to trust. I blamed my husband for the way others misunderstood me.

One horrible encounter happened during what was supposed to be dinner with a married couple who wanted to walk with us through this season. They had been friends with my husband for some years prior to our marriage and, even though their beginning had integrity issues of its own, I believed in redemption and agreed to allow them into our circle. To this day, I will never understand why they postured themselves the way they did that evening, which ultimately severed my ability to ever trust them again.

This couple knew of the challenges in our marriage and minimized it as me being an obsessive, victimized wife who couldn't get over that her husband "masturbated once in awhile." They, like so many others who don't live with addicts and don't see the daily in's and out's, were unable to fathom the depths this sin was taking my husband. How he would take risks and compromise his integrity not only in our marriage, but in his job. How he would completely disconnect from conversations and responsibilities to indulge in his addiction and how that slowly began to change who he was as a person. They neglected to foresee that this addiction would eventually cost him his marriage, his job, friendships, his vehicle, his home, his church, and his walk with God.

Instead, they saw me as insecure and overreacting. They saw me as the problem. The conversation that evening became heated because clearly we had different perspectives. The woman was quiet and allowed her husband to do all the talking. This man became so loud and so angry towards me that his face turned red as he stood up and said (with spit literally flying out of his mouth), "I don't see what the big deal is...men masturbate! Even I masturbate once in awhile!!!" I was mortified! A little TMI and inappropriate. His wife had a look of terror on her face, too. I immediately headed for the door and then to our car.

This man, like so many others, didn't get it. Not all men who masturbate or look at porn become addicted—but my husband was and our life was spiraling out of control. Yet somehow these people didn't see the big deal. I blamed my husband for that man's stance and how he treated me. I screamed and cried in rage all the way home. It was just horrible. Not only was I being rejected by my spouse, but I was being blamed by those around us. The very people who could have breathed life into me and our marriage during that season actually hurt us. I grew bitter and self-protective.

The deep shame and humiliation were compounded when the pastor of this new church (where I would remain for three years) did not seem too concerned about my husband's spiritual condition or what it was doing to me emotionally, spiritually, and eventually physically. I won't make excuses for this pastor, but I do feel the need to say that all of us are fallible, imperfect beings—churchgoers and church leaders. I don't believe this pastor was/is even aware of his actions, but the spiritual abuse I endured under his leadership (or lack thereof) hindered me nonetheless and left me near suicidal.

This church leadership was more concerned about my husband's musical talent and bringing that to their worship team then they were about the seriousness of the depravity that the porn addiction was causing him, our marriage, and me. My husband was frequenting porn and sex shops regularly—all while holding a key to the church doors—because he was in music ministry there. It's so perverse that it's mind-blowing to me and it literally almost was. At one point the pastor suggested that God was after something in me and perhaps it had nothing to do with my husband's porn addiction.

While it is true that God can use someone else's poor choices for our good, twisting the reality of my husband's addiction to sound like God was just after something deeper within me, rather than my husband's depravity, was outright abusive. But I was so broken and already guilt-ridden, embarrassed, and ashamed that I did not stand against this leading. I did not argue it because I thought I needed to "obey spiritual authority" and listen to their counsel. I had been taught someone else's perspective of a scripture in Hebrews and that tape was playing on repeat in my head.

Eventually I became physically sick and at one point had several surgeries that involved my being bedridden and not allowed to have sex for a time so my body could heal. It was suggested by this same pastor that there were "other things" I could do to gratify my husband as my body was healing so that he would not turn to pornography. Once again, a person of influence was leading me to think I had the ability to control my husband's addiction. I was humiliated, hurt, and confused. I needed compassion and rest, but what I was getting was horrible advice and counsel on how to be a good wife to a man who was choosing pornography over everything in his life.

This same pastor later reminded me that I was not to withhold sex from my husband Biblically and that if I was doing that as a means to punish him, then I was in clear disobedience to God. Isn't this just crazy the focus was on me? I was disgusted and I made it known to this pastor (in my husband's presence) that I enjoyed sex. Giving myself to my husband in the bedroom was not a problem I struggled with—in fact, my husband was so dependent upon pornography and masturbation that he was the one who couldn't perform in our marriage bed. That is just the sad truth. But many people don't get this. Many people think if a man is a porn or sex addict that he wants sex (and can perform sexually) all the time. While this may be true for some, statistics will tell you that is not true for the majority.

Evidence increasingly suggests that erectile dysfunction is one of the side-effects of ongoing pornography use. So please don't think that if your husband isn't able to connect with you in the bedroom, then it's because you aren't doing enough or that he doesn't find you attractive. It may very well be because he is suffering the consequences of his own addiction.

And while we're here, let me let you in on something that blew my mind. This is pretty raw and might be TMI for some, but I think it will be helpful to many: men do not have to have an erection to have an orgasm! How do I know this? Because my husband was kind enough to tell me. He knew I blamed myself for his inability to perform in the bedroom. I used to say, "How is it that pornography can have you, but I can't?" He knew the truth. The fact was he didn't have to have an erection with porn to have an orgasm, but he couldn't have intercourse without an erection—hence another reason porn was just easier. He had conditioned his mind, which had physiological consequences of desensitization. Another sad truth.

So, back to the church ordeal I was in. As if the pastor's wasted opportunities to speak truth and wisdom into my life weren't enough of a disappointment, the youth pastor who was buddies with my husband had the nerve to say that I reminded him of Eve in the garden. And that my disobedience in submission was why our marriage was not healing. The context of that conversation came after one of many separations when I refused to allow my husband to come back home without any fruit of repentance in his life.

I finally broke free of this ignorant pastor and his leadership through the permission I received from a Christian counselor who suggested that this was spiritual abuse (something I had never heard a term for) and he feared for my sanity and my relationship with God if I didn't get out of there. That counselor may never know that he saved my life that day.

Finally we found another small church. But once again, an ill-equipped (though well-meaning) leadership welcomed us. A young pastor and his wife would certainly be more understanding of the reality we were facing or so I thought. After a few months there, when I felt safe enough to confide in the pastor's wife about some of the situations I was facing and what exactly my husband was doing. She actually freaked out; she did not want "her mind to be tainted by things that were impure." I am dead serious— that was her reaction. She chose to bury her head in the sand rather than walk through the darkest days of my life with me. Another blow to my rejected and defeated heart.

Ironically we were in that church right around the time I was volunteering for XXXchurch. That pastor thought it was a mistake for me to be serving a ministry that was "so close to this addiction." I prayed about it and was confident this was where God called me. Had I "submitted" to his thoughts about my involvement with XXXchurch, my role with Recover and this book would be non-existent today. I know that God had a plan in the midst of it all—taking into account the choices of our free will—and yet He still worked it out for my good. As a matter of fact, it was my boss and his wife who stepped up to the plate and cared for me where others should have, but didn't during the darkest season of my life.

So dear one, if this is you, if you find yourself feeling isolated and without a solid support system in your church or friendships that can speak life and encouragement to you, let me give you permission to **FIND NEW ONES.**

I'm not suggesting church-hopping when you don't get the answers you want in the time frame you want them. I *am* suggesting that you prayerfully weigh and consider it all. I was in that first church for three solid years—submitting the best I could to the counsel I was being given, trusting the Lord even if I was broken and imperfect. God rescued me out of that situation and if you are not where you need to be, trust that He will rescue you, too. Just be open to what that might look like.

I am not sharing this with you to bash churches, pastors, or people. That would be counterproductive here. All the things I've shared happened long before the road was paved to even talk about porn in church. Churches are much more equipped today to walk with people struggling with addiction. I love a healthy church that has healthy (even if flawed) leadership. My reason for sharing this is because if there is a woman out there going through the same things I went through, then I want her to know she has a choice. God is not going to be disappointed in her if she can no longer submit herself to ill-equipped people in her church or in her life. She will not suffer a curse for taking care of herself! The Bible tells us in several places to pursue peace. Don't forget that. You can't be at peace if the people in your life don't support you and point you to wholeness and well-being.

I pursued healing and wholeness at all costs. I lost some friends and even family members for staying in the marriage as long as I did. I lost some of the things that meant the most to me, one being the house I wanted and worked for my whole life. Dreams that were intercepted by addiction in marriage. I also lost a brother and sister-in-law and their kids whom I loved and adored for over a decade, but who would remain loyal to their sibling and silently disappear from my life.

But in spite of loss, I was determined to find healing regardless of whether or not my husband ever did. Whether or not I had the support of the people I loved the most. I made a lot of mistakes in my marriage, especially early on and I needed opportunities to make those things right for my own conscience's sake. Perhaps that is why I stayed as long as I did.

The truth is, my marriage did not survive this addiction. I hung in there longer than most ever will and honestly, I didn't have to. I know my story is one that no one wants.

Heck, I didn't want this to be my story! But there was still purpose to be found in it and I believe the things I learned in those years can help you and others.

My marriage did not end because of a lack of love for my husband or a lack of faith in God. My marriage ended because my husband ultimately chose his pornography addiction over our marriage and I finally said enough is enough (for me). He didn't just look at porn (relapse) randomly throughout the years. Porn was a constant. The longest it wasn't in the middle of our marriage was a 2 month stretch.

Instead, it was many years of interventions and offerings from pastors, friends, and family to help him/us. Even after several counselors (pastoral, Biblical, and psychological) as well as a nine-month live-in program for men bound by sex addiction— he still chose to leave our marriage repeatedly for days at a time or months of separations. His only goal was to pursue isolation with pornography (and only God knows if there was more).

He would return home each time as a shadow of someone I once knew until there was nothing left of the man I married. He was unrepentant and, as of the writing of this book, he remains that way. By his own admission, he doesn't attend church or pray anymore. I don't hate my soon-to-be-ex-husband—my heart is broken for him and I will pray for him until I no longer have breath, but I cannot align myself or my life up with a man who has abdicated his role as my husband and turned his face against God. Some may argue that he is just filled with lust and is feeding his flesh, but I honestly believe he is using porn to medicate indescribable pain in his life. Until he believes that and seeks to heal the pain in healthy ways, he will remain bound.

I have seen countless marriages survive and come back stronger than they ever were before the discovery of betrayal, so do not think for one moment that, because my marriage didn't survive, yours doesn't have a chance. There is always hope. After all—look at the six other ladies on the Recover.org project. All their marriages have survived (and thrived!) to this day. And they are only a handful of the many we've come to know who are living an abundant life with their spouses in victory over sexual sin.

You may be thinking, "But where is the hope for those whose marriages don't make it? Where is their hope in her story?!" And my response is this: There is so much hope in my story. What was once broken, bitter, and unrecognizable is now redeemed, raised up, and polished with purpose and calling. Anyone can be happy when they get what they want—but to possess true joy, peace, and contentment when you don't get the outcome you want and you've lost what was most valuable to you, now that is being **Recovered by Hope!** And I believe with all of my heart that, as long as my husband has breath, there is hope for a conscious awakening and for his redemption.

One of the most helpful things that brought about healing in my journey has been serving others. Even in the midst of my brokenness, God could use me and in that I would be strengthened too. Serving others wasn't always directly serving people. There were many years I was too broken for that, but I could serve at local animal shelters and rescue organizations where I walked dogs and cleaned cages. I could serve the church by folding church bulletins or making a meal for a family who was going through an illness. Eventually I could serve others by holding babies and playing with small children in the church nursery or chaperoning teenagers at local youth events. Ultimately I could serve others by sharing my journey with other women so they would know they were not alone.

One of the greatest gifts (aside from Christ) that God has given to all of us is His creation. I love nature, the ocean, and anything scenic, really. I have a hobby for photography and love to venture out and just spend hours upon hours capturing some of the beauty in the earth. There was a time when I thought I was so debilitated from the pain of betrayal and my own shameful responses that I just didn't feel like doing anything. But I learned to pursue the things that once brought me joy even when I didn't feel like it and eventually those experiences changed me and helped catapult me to a place of gratitude, a place of peace, and a place of hope for the future.

For me, through all of this, I now know the love of a Father that I've never known before. One that, in spite of any poor choices I've ever made, calls me His own and pursues my heart daily. I have the love of my amazing grown children and now three beautiful grandchildren with an opportunity to speak life and well-being into their lives. I have a solid support system in place and I know I can stand on my own; no matter what happens in this life, God will always provide for me. He will never forsake me and He can be trusted. Only HE is eternal. The things in this earth, including marriage, are not.

My healing didn't happen overnight and surely it wasn't dependent on whether my spouse ever found victory over addiction. My healing is ongoing, but it is happening through an intentional pursuit of wholeness. It is happening through many victories *and* failures. It is happening through choosing to look past my circumstances and into the eyes of a loving God who knows me by name and tells me I am His and He has good plans for me.

He has good plans for you, too.

BE WELL,
MICHELLE

To watch more of Michelle's story, visit Recover.org.

WE HAVE THIS
HOPE AS AN ANCHOR
FOR THE SOUL,
FIRM & SECURE.
IT ENTERS THE INNER
SANCTUARY BEHIND
THE CURTAIN,
WHERE OUR
FORERUNNER,
JESUS, HAS ENTERED
ON OUR BEHALF.

- Hebrews 6:19-20 NIV

If you have a story of hope as it relates to recovering from sexual betrayal or if this book has spoken to your heart, we'd love to hear from you.

———————

Email us: stories@recover.org

ACKNOWLEDGEMENTS

Thank you to my mother, Cathryn. In writing this book I have gained much more appreciation for you. Thank you for choosing to give me life in a world that was suggesting otherwise. You suffered many betrayals and rejections of your own. May you know and believe that God loves you and has not wasted one ounce of your suffering. I am living proof.

Thank you to my son, David. Born to an unwed teenage mom who knew nothing about life or parenting. You suffered many consequences of my choices and yet always chose forgiveness and grace, somehow still calling me your hero. You truly are the best thing that has ever happened to me.

Thank you to the people who helped shaped my life: Dayle Sigmund, Fred & Pat Duncan, The Moseley family, Joy Thomas, John & Ellen Duke, and Sally Jeffery. Each of you have poured something significant into me—your investment has helped me to become all I was meant to be.

Thank you to Craig Gross. There are no words for the love and gratitude in my heart for you. You have given your life to ministry so that others could find theirs. You have been a generous boss, a compassionate friend, and have walked alongside me on this journey. You helped me to believe that something good would come from my story.

Thank you to Jesus. In the midst of brokenness, you were intricately weaving it all together—bringing purpose from the pain. You have taught me so much about love, grace, and second chances. Thank you for choosing me and never regretting it.

Made in the USA
Columbia, SC
24 April 2017